NEVER KNEW

I

WAS

A

DINOSAUR

A Memoir

NEVER
KNEW
I
WAS
A
DINOSAUR

A Memoir

Glenn Sartori

This book is memoir. It reflects the author's present recollections
of experiences over time. Some names and characteristics have
been changed, some events have been compressed, and some
dialogue has been recreated.

First edition published by Enigma Books, an imprint of Prince
and Pauper Press, Clinton, MI.

Paperback ISBN: 978-1-62251-046-7

Other Books by Glenn Sartori

Novels:

Epiphany
Union of Friends
Consequences of Falling
The Triplets' Secret

South City Mosaic Memoirs:

Life on Alaska
Life on South Grand
Life on West Pine

DEDICATION

To the employees of the electronics company in
Building 500, St. Charles, MO.
Remembering our years together: unique, unrivaled
and never to be duplicated.

And in memory of my workmates, Joel Germeroth
and Bob Putman—fellow engineers, Bridge partners,
and all-around good guys.

CONTENTS

Introduction..11

In the beginning..13

The horrific crash...19

The badge..23

The pocket protector..29

The slide rule and other technological dinosaurs......33

Secretaries and the heaviest memo.............................39

The transistor club..45

No escaping your boss...49

The cube farm and its inhabitants...............................53

Carpooling...59

Qualification tests and those who loved them...........63

Let's go a soldering...69

Six sigma...73

Bowling at the corner bar..79

Immersion...83

The nightclub..89

Supervisors—the good and the bad...........................95

Building 500..99

The picnics aka reunions..105

Traveling for the man..109

10-4 good buddy..117

In conclusion..121

Acknowledgements..125

About the author..126

INTRODUCTION

I hate introductions... maybe this one is brief.

Like you, my dear reader, I'm not a fan of long introductions in non-fiction books, they're typically preachy, and I usually skim most of them. No fears, this one is short, to the point, and without pontificating.

Okay, let's get to it.

My book is not about the dinosaurs that roamed the earth in prehistoric times or those reanimated in *Jurassic Park*, but about human dinosaurs.

When someone labels a person a dinosaur, what does that usually mean?

I'm sure you know, but I thought I'd write it down. That label is for a person who hangs on to a dying technology, wears outdated clothing styles, or uses conversational terms from eons ago. Maybe you know some other attributes that might tag a person a dinosaur.

Anyway, some are oblivious to the fact they are dinosaurs, while others carry it like a badge of honor. People don't start out in their teenage years, work lives or professional careers, or golden years planning to be a dinosaur. I absolutely did not.

How does a person become a dinosaur? Do you know any dinosaurs?

Hmm... Fred, my neighbor, does this thing...

Wait! Don't tell me. That's your story, for your memoir.

My memoir offers a humorous look at dinosaur activities, dinosaur fixations, prehistoric technologies, and yes, my dinosaur behaviors. It spans my professional career as an electronic engineer in the high-tech business world. You might think that stories of company goings-on would be dull and dry—maybe some are, but many are not. I'm sure you have seen absurdity and humor in jobs you've had. I certainly have in mine.

Anyway, I hope you turn the page and enjoy reading about my workplace adventures, and maybe you'll recognize some dinosaur mannerisms in yourself or your friends. By the way, being a dinosaur is not necessarily a bad thing, although many might view it as odd, but some consider it quaint.

* * *

Warning! Uh, oh, maybe *warning* is too strong a word for my announcement. Maybe *alert* is better. Or is *heads-up* the correct word?

Wait! What are you doing? You've ended the introduction already. What is this?

When my editor gently pointed out that I overuse the word *anyway*, I searched my manuscript, and she was right. But I like it. And I thought, so what if it's in nearly all of the chapters, it's an excellent segue.

So… after you have read my memoir, and if you were annoyed by the frequency of the *anyways*, send me your name, address, phone number, date of birth and social security number, and I'll happily refund you the cost of the book.

IN THE BEGINNING

Oh no, how far is this guy going back?

You'll be relieved to know that this book does not start with the creation of earth, like a James Michener novel typically does; mine starts with my first real job.

I'll admit that I've accomplished some small things in my life. I certainly didn't start a billion-dollar company or a world-changing nonprofit, but I had an exciting, rewarding, sometimes humorous, career in the high-tech electronics industry and loved it.

Starting a new job is an exciting time, a fresh beginning, and the beginning of an adventure—you're not sure what's around the corner—and on that first day, you don't know if you'll be there a year later, years later, decades later, or if you'll want to quit before the first day ends.

In 1962, I reported for work at the McDonnell Aircraft Corporation in St. Louis, Missouri. I wore the same dark suit I wore at my college graduation. The suit was my parents' gift to me. I was so excited when my mom told me we were going to Southtown Famous-Barr—the place-to-shop in the South City of St. Louis—to buy a suit.

It had a single-breasted jacket with two buttons and a single-vent in the back. I wore a white shirt, and skinny dark tie—not as cool looking as *Don Draper* on the TV program *Mad Men*, but still cool. I was a newly minted electrical engineer—young and naïve but full of ideas, energy and a desire to work—all set to jump into the world of hi-tech electronic design.

My career spanned forty years, one month and twenty-eight days at the same company.

Really?

Yep. You read that right—the same company. Who does that anymore? No one. I'm the last of a dying breed, maybe heading for a place in history. Lengthy careers at the same company are definitely headed for extinction—like what happened to the dinosaurs.

Speaking of dinosaurs, they walked the earth over 165 million years ago and lived during a time-period known as the Mesozoic Era. Over the years, their numbers dwindled due to cataclysmic events, falling asteroids, and wild environmental changes, finally becoming extinct at the end of the Cretaceous Period —that was around 65 million years ago—although the micro-raptors…

Wait! That was too much dinosaur talk and quite unnecessary.

You are right. This book is not about those kind of creatures. You probably know that by now… you did read the introduction, didn't you?

Similar to some dinosaurs, I survived company-generated asteroids—layoffs, reductions in the force, downsizing, right sizing—all euphuisms for we need to fire some people.

Anyway, back to youthful me. My first day at McDonnell Aircraft was on a Monday, June 4, 1962, less than a month out of college—an electrical engineering degree in my name, a slide rule in one hand and my brown bag lunch in the other. I was ready to make some real money.

Real money was $350 a week.

At the age of twenty-two, I started in the Electronic Equipment Division (EED), assigned to a gray metal desk—all desks were the same, apparently salvaged from some military outpost—in a bullpen, on the mezzanine of Building 101.

First, a couple of things:

Number one: A bullpen is a setup where employees work at desks on an open floor with no partitions separating them. You may have seen these layouts in newsrooms and detective offices in the movies or on TV. It was a great arrangement for eavesdropping on business and personal conversations and having zero privacy. Engineers, who took a drag from their cigarettes, blew smoke toward the yellowing ceiling-tiles, considerate, and some engineers left the bullpen to pick their noses.

Number two: Each building in the McDonnell complex was numbered, where Building 1 was the company headquarters... so in the building pecking-order, mine was near the bottom. However, the ground floor of Building 101 was the assembly area for the Gemini 9 Spacecraft, nice view from my desk on the mezzanine. Pretty cool, huh?

Project Gemini was NASA's second human spaceflight program. It followed the Mercury Project and was in preparation for the Apollo Program and the moon landings. The Gemini spacecraft carried a two-astronaut crew. Gemini 7 spent nearly fourteen days in space, making a total of two hundred and six orbits.

That was a boring tech blurb.

Okay. I apologize for that, but I couldn't resist inserting some history. There are others scattered in this book, so... in subsequent chapters I'll add a note indicating a tech blurb is next, and you can skip it if you wish. But I hope you don't. But you still can. But I hope you don't.

Remember, you are, of course, fully in control of what you choose to read, and may pass over any chapter of this book at will. No pressure, but don't scan over too many chapters or you'll miss some good laughs.

Really? No pressure?

Anyway, I worked for the same company for my entire engineering career; however, I did change buildings, lived through organizational changes—*re-orgs* as we called them—and rounds of various company leaders. To me, most re-orgs seemed illogical. The *Dilbert* cartoon strip seemed to agree, it mocked those changes and other company foolishness. Scott Adams, the creator of *Dilbert*, always seemed to know current corporate trends.

Many times, I was in nomad-mode, boxing up my personal and business items for the company movers to transfer me to a different location in the same building or to another building on the sprawling campus. Rumor was that five percent of the McDonnell workforce was always moving—it saved money, the company needed less desks.

Huh?

By the way, that packing skill benefited me in my home life. I enjoy boxing gifts for shipments to out-of-town family and friends. I take pride in choosing the smallest box size, arranging the gifts inside, and using commercial-grade tape to seal the package. I'm good at it as validated by postal workers who have given me kudos.

Ahhhh.

Could you please cover your mouth when you yawn?

Anyway, the dinosaurs adapted to changes in their surroundings but struggled when meteors began to pummel the earth. Things exploded around me as I did my job, but I focused on the tasks, worked with new crops of employees, and enjoyed my assignments along the way. I adapted to the goings-on above me, not a difficult thing to do until the day of... The Merger.

With lead-in music, that would've sounded like a line from The Days of our Lives.

Nevertheless, leading up to that fateful day, other corporate changes occurred...

Five years after I started work, McDonnell Aircraft merged with Douglas Aircraft and became McDonnell Douglas Corporation (MDC) in 1967.

Mergers and Acquisitions were in the air.

I didn't think that M&A's would affect me, but they did. MDC acquired Conductron Corporation of Ann Arbor, Michigan, in exchange for stock and the personnel and equipment of my division. I was like a baseball player traded to an expansion team. I now worked for Conductron-Missouri.

Who?

You and everyone else asked the same question.

My new home was on North Third Street in St. Charles, Missouri, in the former Sterling Aluminum Company building—labeled Building 500. Talk about low building pecking-order. However, I did graduate from a bullpen to a cube farm—an office workspace in which employees work in cubicles with five-foot-high walls.

Then came the era of combining operations, splitting them apart, and then recombining. That business nonsense was in fashion and all the rage among corporate America. MDC ascribed to that philosophy. My company became the Electronics Division of the MDC Astronautics Company.

Wow, that rolls off your tongue.

Exactly. Did it make any sense? Absolutely not. I was in the same building, at the same desk, doing the same job… only difference—a new leader signed my paycheck. That organizational structure was doomed to disband, and it did.

Less than two years later, we became McDonnell Douglas Electronics Company (MDEC)—our own company with our own president. We had arrived. We were big timers now. I spent most of my career—great times and challenging jobs—in Building 500 with a myriad of new products to design and build. I even graduated to an office with a door and had a secretary. I was living the good life.

All of that fun ended on July 31, 1997, when (cue the music) *The Merger* materialized. It wasn't really a merger, but an outright purchase of MDC by Boeing. The Boeing Corporation assimilated MDC personnel into different buildings, different divisions, and a different culture. Luckily, I remained in St. Louis with my team—avionic and ground support equipment—relatively intact. I was thrilled. This happened because Boeing had a similar group in Seattle but much smaller than mine in St. Louis—none of those Seattle people moved here. Their loss.

My final move was to Building 102, the next-door neighbor of my first building—it was the circle of life, but not quite as dramatic as in the *Lion King*.

Then I retired on July 31, 2002, and I'm enjoying every moment of it.

THE HORRIFIC CRASH

Oh my, do I want to know?

I wanted to share this story but was unsure of where to place it in the book. It was a dreadful tragedy that happened years ago, although maybe some of you have heard about it. I am recounting the story not because I wish to be gruesome, but because it made an impression on me and is still with me today.

I had been working for McDonnell Aircraft for less than four years when it happened. I was in Building 102, a short walk from my building, in a second-floor conference room, attending a morning project meeting when the crash occurred.

It was Monday, February 28, 1966, around 9 a.m.

Two astronauts Elliott See Jr. and Charles Bassett II were flying from Houston to St. Louis for training in a visual and mechanical simulator. They were the lead crew for Gemini 9—the blastoff scheduled for May 1966—and their space capsule was to rendezvous with a satellite. Bassett was to execute a spacewalk, all part of the preparation for a moon landing. They never made that space flight.

Everyone at the meeting in Building 102 heard the roar and the crash. We hurried to the window to see billowing smoke and flames rising in the air. What had happened? I had a sickening feeling. I knew it was bad.

We rushed outside, acrid air stung my nose as I watched smoke curl toward the sky. Company security met us on the sidewalk and told us to go back inside. For the rest of the workday, I stayed in Building 102, where very little was accomplished as news reports and rumors circulated throughout the area.

Fog and rain engulfed St. Louis Lambert Airport. Astronaut Elliott See, piloting their NASA T-38 military training jet, approached too high and began a tight swing around the airport. He radioed to fellow astronauts, Thomas Stafford and Eugene Cernan, flying miles behind them in another T-38. He said that he was preparing for a visual landing on the airport's diagonal runway, close to the McDonnell complex. His T-38 clipped the roof of Building 101 with its right wing. The fuselage skipped twice across the roof, plunged into a construction yard and exploded. (Stafford and Cernan didn't see the crash and made an instrument landing fourteen minutes later.)

By noon the following day, I was back in Building 101. Fortunately, only seventeen people inside the building sustained injury and that was from falling ceiling debris. None seriously, none of whom I knew. And my area looked as if nothing had happened. The gory details of the crash and pictures of the crash site headlined the newspaper and consumed the local and national TV news. Both astronauts died instantly from trauma sustained in the crash. Pilot See was thrown clear of the cockpit and was found in the parking lot still strapped to his ejection seat with the parachute partially open, and co-pilot Bassett was found in the wreckage still buckled in his seat.

Astronauts See and Bassett died within five hundred feet of the Gemini spacecraft that was supposed to take them into orbit.

Flags at every McDonnell building flew at half-mast.

Alan Shepard and Deke Slayton, two of the original seven Mercury astronauts, flew to St. Louis to lead the investigation. Building 101 was the location for the closed enquiry—throughout the building, although not on the mezzanine where I worked. On May 27, their report cited deteriorating weather conditions and a descent that was too steep for pilot Elliott See to pull out.

That was the most tragic event in the original NASA space missions.

However, like any huge project, the NASA space program had to go on—the Gemini Mission continued. The original May 17th launch had been scrubbed, and the mission renamed Gemini 9A. On June 3rd, a Titan II rocket blasted Astronauts Stafford and Cernan, the backup crew, into orbit inside their spacecraft. The mission went smoothly. Cernan walked in space for one hundred and twenty-nine minutes.

In those early days of my career, I was fortunate and thrilled to have a front row seat in the construction and testing of space capsules and was able to shake hands with some of the original astronauts.

THE BADGE

Are you talking about a police badge?

No. I'm not talking about the insignia badges worn by police, sheriff, firemen or other oval, five-starred or shield-styled emblems. I'm talking about identification badges, IDs—plain, usually plastic and rectangular.

Probably back in prehistoric times, Neanderthals needed some kind of identification to enter a cave, maybe it was a specific animal skin, a bone or antler headgear, jewelry made from seashells—or a really big club.

To access McDonnell Aircraft property, you needed a photo ID badge embossed with an employee number. The badge was the ultimate pecking-order insignia. James S. McDonnell, founder and CEO of the corporation, had the employee number—you guessed it—one.

Mine was 700023.

If I had hired into the Aircraft Division, my number would have been 100023, but because I hired into the Electronic Equipment Division (EED), the company added 600000 to it.

Why?

Well, it was not like the *Wheel of Fortune* when Pat Sajak adds $1000 to the final spin dollar amount, which is a good thing. In my case, the added number put me in a segregated group, fringe employees outside the core mission of the company, assigned a new block of badge numbers. The electronics division was a business experiment, like a pharmaceutical company running a new drug trial. Both with the hope that the results would add tons of dollars to the bottom line.

The EED badge numbers began with either a six or seven and made us easily recognizable as *that* group, which couldn't have been more apparent—unless our foreheads had *loser* tattooed on it.

The cool thing was that we weren't losers, which non-EED engineers implied that we were, prattling on about their importance to the company mission. In fact, we were doing high-tech electronic design work; while other engineers in the company were working on low-tech system designs.

Anyway, back to the employee badges.

I was close to being the one hundred thousandth employee, only twenty-three off. Who had that milestone number? Surely, that person received some notoriety. Excitement filled me as I began my search to find that person. I furtively glanced at employees' badges as I engaged them in conversation. They probably noticed, but I didn't care—I was on a mission. The closest I found was Bill, a fellow EED engineer, whose badge number was only four greater than the milestone number.

Over coffee, and after some baseball talk, I asked, "Bill, do you know the one hundred thousandth employee?"

"Yeah. Fred McKlusky."

A pulse of energy ran through me. Bill knew him. I had to meet Fred. "Where does he work? Was there big celebration?"

"I ran across him in the machine shop and noticed his badge number. He said that the only fanfare was a free lunch in the executive cafeteria with James McDonnell."

I let Bill's words sink in, then "Now that I think about, it's not that surprising. McDonnell was frugal and labeled the Scotsman. He—."

The company-wide speaker system crackled.

"This is Old Mac calling all the *Team*." Loudspeakers blasted James McDonnell's words throughout every building. It shocked me for a moment. Did he know we were talking about him? No. That's foolishness. "This is Old Mac calling all the *Team*." He always repeated the phrase.

McDonnell's announcement concerned some new business the company received, nothing about Fred McKlusky, the one-hundred thousandth employee. Why should he mention that, it was months ago. Anyway, he ended the announcements as he always did. "This is Old Mac signing off... signing off." That's how the CEO communicated news to the employees in prehistoric days. Yep, no emails back then.

Returning to the subject of badges...

There's more?

Plenty. Besides the employee numbers, the badges were colored-coded to indicate your expertise—green for engineering, yellow for purchasing, blue for contracts, yada, yada, yada. Engineering-based companies love color-coding, but that system did not extend to EED. This was another chance for the company to enhance our segregation—*every* employee in the electronic division had a bronze-colored badge. The color was brown, but we called it bronze, which sounded more important since the company's big-timers had either gold or silver badges—pecking-order personified.

At some point in time, somebody felt sorry for us or decided that the company IDs should be uniform and changed the color of our badges to indicate the person's skill, thus in line with the rest of the company. My badge was green—the color for engineers.

Then it got weird.

Supervisors' badges became bi-colored, probably an idea of a deranged person in the Human Resources department. The HR department always came up some bizarre change to validate its existence. For engineering supervisors, the badge was half-green and half-silver. The pecking-order gods were well pleased.

That split-colored badge led to a prank.

That sounds like you're drifting off topic... but it may be interesting.

In our group of about thirty engineers, there was one, who was over-the-top status conscious. Let's call him Roger. There was another engineer, who was on the prankish side—a kind label since some of his pranks bordered on bullying. Let's call him Norris.

One morning, Norris brought in a stack of peel-off labels. He didn't share with us where he'd gotten them, but when a need arose, he seemed to have access to every imaginable service. You probably guessed it—the labels were green and silver. He handed one to every engineer, except Roger. (We knew what to do with them.) His message was— *at eleven on the dot, walk by Roger's cubicle, say good morning, and display your badge with a flourish.*

Why did we follow Norris in this middle-school prank? Because Roger was not only a status seeker, but also annoying, an egotistical nitpicker, and an all-around irritant. A description shared by all, and one Roger didn't seem to mind, in fact he flaunted it. I've always wondered why.

Anyway, I was apprehensive, not one-hundred percent on board, but...

Concentrating on work that morning took a focused effort. I became a clock-watcher. Timing was important. Synchronization was key, and Norris used an old nerd phrase—*simonize your watches.*

I smiled when I wrote that phrase in my draft of this book. It's a dinosaur thing.

The wall clock second-hand clicked toward eleven, sounding like the countdown to a spacecraft launch. Then, an eternity later, the hands indicated eleven o'clock.

The line of faux-supervisors paraded by Roger's cube. We were like munchkins, all in step, smiling, swinging our badges as we passed his cube opening, and wishing him a good morning. It was middle-school antics in the hi-tech business world.

As I approached Roger's cube, heaviness filled my body, my chest tightened. Apprehension packed the air. When I was at the cube opening, Roger seemed shocked, but soon our laughter gave the prank away. He stood and yelled, "Norris!" He pushed through the line, hurried to the department manager's office to inform our leader—an employee with an official green and silver badge—of his mistreatment.

By the way, eventually, Roger and I did become engineering supervisors and exchanged our green badges for the official half-green, half-silver badge. It seemed anti-climactic.

Oh, I forgot to mention there were badge rules...

How long is this chapter?

Rule #1: Always have your badge visible when at work.

Rule #2: Never set your badge down.

Rule #3: Do not display your badge when out in public.

Rule #4...

Wait! Rule number three sounds weird.

Well, it's not that weird. During my years at the company, the cold war was going strong—United States versus Russia. Newspapers, magazines, and TV covered the border standoffs, missile crises, and hot spots around the globe. You couldn't escape the news. Even the Beatles got into it with their *Back in the USSR* song in 1968.

Wearing your badge off company premises announced that you worked at a hi-tech company. Seeing that, a Russian spy could approach you. You might be offered money for company secrets, blackmailed for company secrets, or worst be kidnapped and tortured for a company secret. Could happen. Didn't you watch the awarding-winning TV series *The Americans*?

I am proud to have been an engineer, working in the electronics field, and my badge validated that. But I was a rule-follower and removed my badge as soon as I left the company premises. For nostalgic reasons, I wish I had my company badge today, but when I retired, I had to turn it in—part of the exit interview.

THE POCKET PROTECTOR

What's a pocket protector?

I thought someone might ask that.

A pocket protector is a sheath that fits inside the breast pocket of a shirt—an engineer's necessity and a cool fashion statement.

When I hired into McDonnell Aircraft, the employee badge was displayed one of two ways—clipped to your clothing, but that was for losers—or slid into the clear plastic pouch on the front of the pocket protector. The protector also held writing instruments (pens and pencils—you remember those things) and other items such as a small screwdriver and a six-inch metal ruler.

Huh?

Don't worry about that.

Anyway, the protector shielded the wearer's shirt pocket from tearing (when a pen is pulled from the pocket in a hurry) or from staining by a leaky pen. And a flap overlapping the pocket exterior helps to secure the pocket protector in place.

The protector provided a great opportunity for advertising, with the flap imprinted with the company's logo, and it has long been associated with engineers. In the olden days, the word engineer conjured up images of guys in short sleeve white shirts, dark ties, glasses taped together at the bridge and "high-water" pants. Within the profession, we knew better—we didn't dress that way, and the pocket protector was simply a practical item to preserve the integrity of our white shirts. I wore mine proudly.

Here's a bit of history for those who care. I did the research, so please read it.

Hurley Smith invented the original pocket protector during the Second World War. He earned a Bachelor of Science in Electrical Engineering in 1933 from Queens University in Kingston, Ontario. While working as an engineer, Smith was concerned about the ink and pencil stains and the fraying around the edges of his shirt pocket.

He made thin rectangles from stiff clear colorless plastic, folded it twice, once approximately in half and once on one end to produce a flap that would extend over the top edge of the shirt pocket. From the side, it looked like a check mark, unsealed at the sides, but wide enough to fit into a shirt pocket with the back extending high enough to protect the back of the pocket and shirt above, and the flap fitting over the front of the pocket. The US Patent Office awarded him Patent # 2417786 for the "Pocket Shield or Protector," filed 3 June 1943, Issued: 18 March 1947.

Well, that was a bit windy, but sort of interesting.

There was a lot more pocket protector history… but I spared you. You're welcome.

Anyway, I wore my pocket protector every day—inside were two pens and a red pencil, and in the outer flap was my badge. Some engineers stuffed it to the breaking point like George Costanza's wallet on the TV program *Seinfeld*.

The pocket protector held my badge until another

status symbol emerged—the lanyard. Just in case you need a definition…

I don't.

A lanyard is a cord or strap worn around the neck, shoulder, or wrist to carry such items as keys or identification cards.

Initially, the lanyards were about a half-inch wide, made of white braided material, and printed with the company name and logo. Soon other lanyards came onto scene—emblazoned with the name of a vendor, a product or a conference; each engineer wore it like a certificate of honor. Their popularity seemed to have exploded overnight and the wilder the color, the more impressive.

Like all of the engineers, I collected lanyards, which I stuffed into a desk drawer. I changed lanyards daily like when I wore a different tie every day to work before every day became causal Friday. It was lanyard-mania. People would swish past you, their lanyard flying in the air, advertising that they had a new lanyard. Some engineers hung the lanyards on their cubicle walls like awards or trophies, and you guessed it, Roger, the local irritant, was one of the first to do that.

Today, lanyards are the go-to badge holder for many businesses. And in case you're interested, pocket protectors are still a thing. Amazon sells them—two for $8.88. They come in leather for a real fashion statement but do not have that cool pouch for your badge.

THE SLIDE RULE AND OTHER TECHNOLOGICAL DINOSAURS

Yeah, I know... Technology moves forward. Keep up or become a dinosaur.

The cutting-edge technology I used during my career is dinosaur technology today. But looking back at those engineering tools, I realized they were pretty cool and did a fine job. So... I thought I'd share a few of them with you.

The Slide Rule...

William Cox of the United States patented the slide rule in 1890. The nineteenth century! Who would have guessed? That's like prehistoric times. Fun fact: That was the same year that Wyoming and Idaho became the 43rd and 44th states.

That was not a fun fact.

The slide rule, or the *slipstick* as engineers lovingly called it, was usually constructed of plastic and consisted of three parts—the main body of the rule, known as the stock, the movable part, known as the slide, and a movable plastic cursor. It calculated multiplication and division problems, trigonometry functions, powers and roots, logarithms, and other exotic engineering formulas. If you want to know more, google it.

The K & E (Keuffel & Esser) Corporation had the honor of producing the last slide rule in July of 1976 and donated it to the Smithsonian Institute. Despite the end of slide-rule manufacturing, you can be sure that many are still in engineers' desks or in their cubes today.

Yep, you guessed it. I still have my slide rule. It was a thing of beauty—a Nestler No. 0290, made in Germany, housed in a leather Gramercy case. My case is now worn and split, and in the yellowing plastic ID window, there still is a card with my name, my home address on Alaska Avenue, and my family's phone number PL 2-2258. Many of my readers of… hmm… a certain age, probably remember their first home phone number. By the way, the alphanumeric system was retired in the late 1950s for a very simple reason: telephone operators often misheard similar sounding letters and connected callers to the wrong numbers.

You drifted off topic again… but it was interesting.

While researching data for this chapter, I held my slide rule, moving the center scale back and forth, trying to imagine using it at work. Nothing. I had no idea how to use it—that knowledge was lost in antiquity, and I wasn't going to relearn it. Sadly, I inserted the slide rule back into its sheath and returned it to its resting place—a bookcase in the basement. Who cares about the slide rule, when the cure for any thirst of knowledge is only a screen-tap or mouse-click away?

The Handheld Calculator…

In September 1971, the Bowmar Company produced the first handheld calculator. It could compute four arithmetic functions—Add, Subtract, Multiply and Divide—and the public fondly labeled it the *Bowmar Brain*. The display was eight LED digits—red numbers that were almost legible. It retailed for about three hundred bucks.

A bit of history…

In three years, Bowmar became the largest manufacturer of handheld calculators in the world. However, with the dramatic decline in calculator prices, Bowmar couldn't keep up with the competition and filed for bankruptcy protection early in 1975.

To the point, but boring

I got my first electronic handheld calculator in 1972. It was the powerful Texas Instruments TI-2500, a four-function beauty, and a competitor of Bowmar. It retailed for $99.95, but with the company discount, I paid twenty-five bucks. Excitement filled me as I used it at every opportunity, even for those calculations I could do in my mind. However, as with any electronic device, it became a dinosaur in less than a year. My desire to have the latest tech gadgets moved me to a multifunction-scientific calculator. I used it constantly until the computer burst onto the company scene in mid-1980s—the Macintosh, a personal computer with a built-in screen.

Today, handheld calculators are still for sale—you can buy a 300-function device for less than fifteen dollars!

The Overhead Projector…

For meeting presentations, I used the overhead projector, which had a light and optics to project an enlarged image onto a screen. In the overhead projector, the source of the image was a page-sized sheet of transparent plastic film with the words either printed or hand-written on it. Currently, you can buy a projector on Amazon for about two-hundred and fifty dollars. But who cares?

The light source—a bulb to my technically challenged readers—emitted a lot of heat, fine on cold day, but not so fine for a nervous presenter. Well aware of Murphy's Law—if the bulb burns out, it will burn out in the middle of a presentation—we had a spare nearby. Good thinking, huh? And since the bulb was extremely hot, we used gloves to replace it... we didn't actually use gloves; we took a coffee break till it cooled down.

My first ever overhead presentation was one slide—a matrix that listed circuit boards and the electronic components on them. Yep, a prehistoric spreadsheet. Engineers love spreadsheets. I sweated over drawing the matrix on the slide, I drew the lines using a ruler and the black marker. I trashed many slides before I got it right, then wrote numbers in each square. It was a thing of beauty. I was ready.

That Friday, we assembled in a conference room to give a status update to the program manager.

"The next slide..." the engineering project manager said, "...is the matrix of the circuit boards and components. Glenn, you're up."

I walked to the projector, placed my slide on the glass, positioning it so that the image on screen was straight. My armpits dampened. "The eight boards—."

"How much do they weigh?" The program manager's question stopped me in my tracks.

I tried not to look shocked even though I was. What kind of question was that? He always seemed to enjoy making presenters squirm with off-the-cuff, generally irrelevant questions. It was common knowledge that he was one of those guys who exemplified Peter's Principle—people in a hierarchy tend to rise to their level of incompetence.

I took a deep breath, exhaled and knew what to say. "The total weight of the black box is twenty-one pounds. I don't know what each board weighs, but I can find out."

"Hmm..." he looked at me, didn't smile, but amazingly didn't look unfriendly, "...next slide."

After the presentation, waves of happiness flowed through me as my team members congratulated me on stumping the program manager. No one respected him.

That was interesting... but you could speed it up.

The next section is the last.

Thank you.

The Pencil...

The pencil is still in use, but not to the level that it was in my working days. If you need a refresher, here it is. A pencil is an implement for writing or drawing, constructed of a narrow, solid graphite core in a protective casing, usually a wood product.

That was an over-the-top definition of a pencil.

Maybe, but... The pencil usage was so high that every engineer had a pencil sharpener, or two. This device allowed you to keep your pencil sharp and to use it down to a stub. We were a thrifty generation. One status-conscious engineer had an electric sharpener... but I won't name him.

Speaking of pencil sharpening...

In 1967, the McDonnell Aircraft Company joined the Douglas Aircraft Company to form... you guessed it—the McDonnell Douglas Corporation. That merger caused signs and logos on company letterheads, property and other items to be changed. One of those items was the pencil, whose new logo resulted in a bizarre anomaly—all company pencils weren't the same.

The west-coast pencils used by the former Douglas employees and the Midwest pencils used by the former McDonnell employees had different etchings. I stumbled upon this fact during a business trip to California. The west-coast pencils had the words McDonnell-Douglas printed from the tip to the eraser end. The Midwest pencils had the opposite—the printing of McDonnell-Douglas was from the eraser end to tip.

So what.

Well, I'll tell you.

If you are on the west coast and sharpen your pencil, the word McDonnell begins to disappear first, and in the Midwest, the word Douglas disappears first.

Back at work, I excitedly told my fellow engineers my discovery. Was that an intentional design? An oversight? A cultural method of stamping pencils?

Their response was—who knows and who cares.

Total agreement here.

Well, I still think it was a cool discovery.

SECRETARIES AND THE HEAVIEST MEMO

Talk about a dinosaur career.

In prehistoric days, secretaries were basically typists, and some companies had a secretarial pool or typing pool. This was a group of women available to assist any employee without an assigned secretary—hidden in a large room, each pounding the keys of their manual typewriter.

When I worked at McDonnell Aircraft, the company employed many secretaries—each department head had one, each program manager had one, and each engineering group had two or three. Scattered throughout a building, they were highly visible and a necessity for a smooth running business.

Rumor had it that the typewriter was built for women— that to truly make the keys hum requires the feminine touch, that their narrow fingers are suited for the device, while men lay claim to planes, trains and automobiles.

That's sexist.

I'm talking about life in the 1960s... cool it.

As the secretaries typed, their fingers seemed to become extensions of their brain, while the keys slapped ink onto paper. And when you think about it, about the mechanics of it all, it's almost poetic... almost, but not quite.

Wait... maybe some of my young readers may have never seen a picture of a typewriter or seen one in a museum. If not, visualize your computer keyboard at angle with each row of keys on a different level. Maybe I should've had a picture.

Oh well, too late now.

Anyway, secretaries typed internal memos and external correspondence, filed papers and reports, and made the coffee. They were eager to satisfy all of the needs of the engineers and supervisors, but typing memos was their main task.

There was a secretary in my engineering group—let's call her Suzie. She was perky to a fault, but a great asset to the team, always willing to pitch in. She not only livened up the office but also held the Guinness record for the heaviest memo.

Heaviest memo?

That's heaviest by weight, not by significance of content.

Huh?

In prehistoric times, when a secretary made a typing mistake, she could throw the paper away and start over with a new sheet or use *Wite-Out*—the correction fluid for typing errors. Description not needed, but the urge to define it is overwhelming. The bottle contained a white liquid, nearly the consistency of nail polish, with a brush mounted in the lid.

I think that was a definition.

Suzie treated the paper as if it were an expensive commodity, didn't throw away any typed-sheets; she brushed *Wite-Out* over the mistake, like a house painter touching up a wall, then she retyped the word. I think you know where this is going.

Not really, but with that lead in, I'm looking forward to reading it.

"Glenn, look at this," a fellow engineer stepped into my

cubicle and handed me a memo. "Suzie just typed it."

"Wow!" I could see the strokes of the *Wite-Out*, but when I held it up to the light, the white liquid covered many words, maybe a third of the memo. "It feels heavy."

"How heavy?"

"Umm… let's weigh this baby," I said as excitement flowed through me—we were on to something, maybe a new category in the Guinness Book of Records. (The publication date of the first Guinness Book of Records was 1955.) "This could be big. Bring a blank sheet of typing paper and meet me in the materials lab."

Our materials lab used precise equipment to determine and measure the characteristics of materials, such as mechanical properties, elemental composition, and other interesting attributes. Most importantly, the lab had ultra-accurate scales.

Fred was the engineer in charge of the lab. He was intense, a no-foolishness kind of guy but this time, he bought into the experiment. He calibrated the scale… was this necessary? We weren't weighing moon rocks. Then he eased the blank typewriter paper on the scale as if his career depended on this measurement. The weight was 4.5 grams.

"Before we weigh Suzie's memo, shouldn't we weigh one without *Wite-Out*?" I asked. "Like a *typical* memo."

Fred patted me on the back and said, "Great idea."

The more measurements the better. Engineers loved data.

Fred stepped over to a row of five-drawer file cabinets—Fred was a packrat. He flipped through a manila folder, seemingly looking for the perfect memo, whatever that was.

"Got it!" He handed it to me. I held it up to the light; it

was pure—no *Wite-Out* had infected this memo.

Fred laid it on the scale. It weighed 10.4 grams, less than a half ounce.

"Okay, let's guess," I said, holding Suzie's memo, moving my hands up and down in a weighing motion.

What do you think it weighed?

I don't know. Let's get the story moving. I have a new novel to read on my Kindle.

Okay, okay.

Fred wanted to bring in more engineers, but I said, "Let's just keep it to the three of us." I was not sure why I felt that way, other than the saying—where four or more gather, stuff leaks out.

We hovered around the scale, staring at the display, as if we were reading a top-secret document.

Suzie's memo weighed 23.1 grams, more than double the weight of Fred's *standard* memo.

"Let's make this official," I said.

The next day, Fred handed me a form, listing the three memo weights, the name of the scale and model number, and three slots for signatures and dates. Fred was the master of forms. If you wanted a form, you went to Fred. The three of us signed it, pleased with our discovery, and Fred filed it. That was the last I saw of the form.

We weighed a few more memos, but the excitement dwindled, interest faded and there was no submittal to Guinness. Although, that story makes for fun conversation while sharing beers with my former workmates.

You'd think that *Wite-Out* would have been like the dinosaurs—ending up in extinction. It hasn't. Even though the digital world presents a grave threat to old-school office markets, students still use the correction fluid for their poster projects and last-minute changes to classroom assignments. *Wite-Out* is also popular...

Wait! There's more? Oh no.

Yes. There are other uses, but I found two of them fascinating.

One: It is used by metalworkers. In particular, one process tries to replicate the strong blades made from the ancient technique for Damascus steel. During the process, the problem is that high carbon steel will weld with milder steels, but by coating the mild steel with *Wite-Out* first, the metals are kept from sticking.

Two: It is popular among wedding planners.

You're making that up.

No, I'm not. Google it. Anyway, picture this—a bride checks herself out one last time in the mirror. Oh no! She sees a smudge of lipstick on her dress. The planner saves the wedding—whipping out a bottle of *Wite-Out* and brushing the fluid over the red mark. The dress looks flawless. Here comes the bride.

THE TRANSISTOR CLUB

This is probably some nerdy engineers' group.

Not really… but who isn't curious about how much your co-workers earn?

What?

At McDonnell Douglas, the annual pay increase was a combination of a cost of living raise and a merit raise. The engineering department head distributed each raise on a small white piece of paper with three numbers—present salary, pay increase and new salary.

The day was Friday, December 21, the last workday before the Christmas break. "Congratulations," Bob, my department manager, said in a flat tone as he laid a piece of paper on my desk, blank side up. The scrap looked as if he had torn it from a sheet of typing paper. Why couldn't he have at least used a 3 x 5 card?

"Thank you." I smiled, then glanced down at the blank piece of paper and couldn't help thinking of the motto for people who lay sod—green side up.

He passed out slips of paper to my bullpen mates, as if he were a dealer at a blackjack table. The process was impersonal and blasé to the point that Bob looked as if he wanted to be doing something else, anything else. I wondered how Bob got his raise, surely more personal than discarding used tissue.

A fluttery, empty feeling filled my stomach. Even

though, I'd only been on the job for six months and expected no raise, I still hoped for something, and he did say congratulations. I turned the paper over, holding it close to my chest like gambler ready to peek at a newly dealt card.

My heart skipped a beat. The numbers were scribbled on the paper, as if he had written it while watching TV. I got something—a four-dollar a week raise. I did the math in my head. My raise was slightly more than a one percent increase, but exactly an increase of a dime an hour. Big whoop. Was that the cost of living? Certainly not a merit raise. But it was something. I glanced at the other engineers, met their eyes—poker faces all around. I wondered how my raise compared to theirs.

Moments later, my phone rang. "Hello?" I answered immediately. There was no caller ID in the 1960s.

"We're recruiting new members for the *Transistor Club*. Are you in?"

"Huh?" I glanced around the bullpen. Many people had phones in their ears. Who was this?

The caller's words, "Meet me outside at twelve hundred hours…" were followed by "…oh, this is Norris." then the disconnect click.

Sounds like a military installation. He couldn't have just said noon?

He could've, but… Anyway, I knew who Norris was but had little dealings with him. I wasn't an initiator of pranks or a supporter of his pranks. But this club didn't sound like a prank. I decided to meet him and find out.

Outside the breeze was brisk, the clouds were low but my anticipation was high. A clique of smokers congregated at the corner of the building, walkers strode along the sidewalks, and Norris approached me at a casual pace.

I wondered what the Transistor Club was as I shook his hand.

"If you tell me what your raise was, I'll give you…" he stopped, obviously seeing my perplexed look. "…oh the Transistor Club is a group of engineers who share their salaries and raises with each other."

I wanted to be part of it, but I asked, "Why?"

"Well…" His voice was barely above a whisper."…to see where your salary increases rank with your peers… your worth, so to speak, and to know what the supervisors know. And for ammunition, when you ask for a raise."

It made sense to me, and always being a joiner, I whispered, "I'm in." And without hesitation, I told him my salary and my increase. Why not? Government employees were paid according to their GS (General Schedule) rating, and the schedule was public knowledge.

The next morning, Norris furtively dropped a sheet of typewriter paper on my desk, blank side up, as if he were passing on company secrets. Well… sort of he was. The paper listed fifteen names with salaries, dollar increases and percentage increase; mine was the last on the list. I quickly scanned the names; they were sorted by hiring date. The two other engineers, who started work six months ago as I did, had the same percentage increase. I was happy about that.

The Transistor Club membership grew until nearly all engineers were in the group; even some outsiders had joined. But over the years, salary data became more transparent—range of rates for engineering grades, company average percentage increases, and national average percentages.

I am proud I was a member of the Transistor Club—a dinosaur, but the bellwether for the transparency of salary data today.

One final note about salary…

Oh no. Isn't this chapter long enough?

Probably, but I wanted to share with you that I witnessed the beginning of the Performance Review era. Pretty exciting, huh? No comparison to the Jurassic era, but still… a milestone in the series of workplace "necessities."

The Performance Review was one of the most frightening and degrading experiences in every employee's life. Once the Reviews were underway, I realized that getting my salary info dropped on my desk was more humane than the Review.

In theory, the process was to be a positive interaction between a supervisor—the coach—and an employee—the player—working together to achieve maximum performance. In reality, the supervisor's objectives were: convince you to work harder, obtain a signed confession of your crimes, and justify your low salary.

But the Transistor Club came to the rescue. We pooled our insights on how to influence the process in our favor. Two ideas bubbled to the top. One: Not only broadcast your accomplishments but also the intangibles, like *thinking about* a project and *mentoring* new engineers. Two: No matter how badly your project screwed up, focus on how much money would have been lost if you'd done something stupid.

The Performance Review is a dinosaur but is still alive today. Good luck to you no matter which side of the Review table you sit. I'm sure you'll survive.

NO ESCAPING YOUR BOSS

Intriguing title. This chapter could be good.

The concept of keeping tabs on employees is the cornerstone of micromanagement. The gold-standard method to check on workers is by *walking about*, which has been around forever, as Fred Flintstone's boss, George Slate, did in dinosaur times.

Today, that notion has been popularized by the TV program, *Undercover Boss*. Each episode features an executive masquerading as an entry-level employee to see what's going on in the company. The ninth season premiered on January 8, 2020.

I've watched that program. It's entertaining.

Anyway, I witnessed supervisors—a euphemism for bosses—walking around, peeping into cubicles with inane questions, and hanging out with the guys at the coffee pot. But those tactics rose to a new level with the introduction of the *pager* into the workplace.

The pager, also known as a beeper, was a wireless telecommunications device that received and displayed alphanumeric or voice messages and was clipped to your belt or settled in your pants pocket. The first pager was patented by Al Gross and was used by New York City's Jewish Hospital starting in 1950. Its primary niche was critical communications.

You snuck in that little historical fact with no fanfare.

In the late 1970s, the electronics company supplied each supervisor with a pager—now there was no place to hide. I was assigned a pager, and I hated it, rarely used it, not that I was trying to hide, I just wanted my personal space. My pager gathered dust on my desk most of the time, but that did not sit well with my two supervisors—the department head and program director. They wanted me at their beck and call.

So... I gave my pager to my secretary, Marie. She answered it and located me if the page was important, otherwise she'd say that I would call right back. Marie was an excellent gatekeeper. The process worked fine—my supervisors didn't complain, as they seemed to only want someone to answer it. Since the pager was the latest tech gadget, the company wanted it to be used whenever possible, even instead of a telephone call.

Well... the pager was the first mobile device.

Yes, but the pager's life was short-lived. With the arrival of email then smartphones, the pager became a prehistoric device in the hi-tech world.

The evolution into email communication was a struggle, some of my workmate dinosaurs insisted that we communicate face-to-face or with secretary-typed memos—nothing like good old paper—similar to the Kindle-versus-paperback arguments of today. But there was no avoiding it, email was here to stay—another tether to your boss that made it harder to escape his whims.

Blame it on old Ray, Ray Tomlinson, a member of the inaugural class inducted into the Internet Hall of Fame. Yes, that is a thing... not a brick and mortar hall, but a virtual hall. He sent the first email in 1971 from one computer to another. Yeah... and he used the infamous @ symbol to separate the names of the sender's and the receiver's computers.

Finally, an interesting blurb.

In the late 1980s, I was at my desk in Building 500, staring into my *huge* nine-inch monitor, built into my company-supplied Macintosh computer. I had just composed my first email. Who was the recipient? What was the content? I wish I could recall. Nevertheless, it was an exciting moment. I maneuvered my mouse to the send icon, clicked, and my first email flew into cyberspace. I embraced electronic communication, as if it were the salvation of the universe. However, the revolution evoked conversations like…

"Did you get my email?"

"No, I didn't. Could you print it out for me?"

And…

"You didn't answer my email."

"It was so long… so many questions. I got tired of reading it, put it aside and I… could you summarize it?"

If you have a computer, email is the lifeblood of your existence, the bane of your life, or somewhere in between. I jumped on the email train and never looked back. I loved the threads of the conversations, the ease of electronic filing and the quick availability to retrieve archived data. Email gave the supervisors more access to the engineers, although to respond you had to be at a computer, it was a buffer of sorts, an excusable delay to responding. It was the glorious era before smartphones and texting.

Today, I have an iPhone and love it, but emails have invaded my device. When I check my inbox, messages from companies hawking their wares and breaking-news bytes swamp the messages from family, friends and volunteer organizations. I'm happy I graduated to a smartphone, not like some of my dinosaur friends who cling to the flip phone. Although the circle of life continues—flip phones are in the midst of a major comeback, but the new foldable models aren't anything like the flip phones of the prehistoric days.

And as it turns out… pagers are not dinosaur devices; they are used in two niche markets.

I bet you're going to tell us.

One: Nearly eighty percent of hospitals still use pagers, according to a recent study in the Journal of Hospital Medicine. Even as consumers shifted away from pagers to two-way texting devices, then to cellphones, then to smartphones, pagers have persisted in hospitals.

Two: Another industry that still widely uses the pager is the illegal drug market. That's right. The traffickers use pagers because the communication links are relatively secure.

Uh, oh, excuse me, my iPhone just chirped. Looks like it's an important message from Amazon.com.

THE CUBE FARM AND ITS INHABITANTS

Are the inhabitants farmers? Yuck, yuck, yuck.
That lame remark doesn't deserve a response.

I was never in jail, but I thought about jail when I was assigned to my first cubicle—a cell-sized area with five-foot walls and a narrow opening. I thought about how I'd fix up my cell in prison. How many pushups would I do? Fortunately, there was no cellmate, only me, and the blank gray walls.

I wasn't alone. The cube farm was a sea of cubicles, and eventually everyone adjusted, realizing we were all in the same boat. Engineering design continued without a hiccup.

Anyway, at the end of a weekly staff meeting, Rich, our department head, said: "We have too many empty cubicles. It raises questions in our customers' minds."

What questions? I wondered.

Rich was pleasant, but a vague kind of guy, who ignored nearly all questions. He was at his Peter Principle level. In case you need a definition—the principle states that people in a hierarchy tend to rise to their level of incompetence.

Another definition? Meriam Webster would be proud of you.

"Why don't we rearrange them into conference rooms?" I offered. "We're always short on conference rooms." I was proud of my suggestion,

"Let's do that," others at the meeting said in unison.

His closed-mouth smile said *that idea sucks*. "I was thinking... each one of you should adopt an empty cube and decorate it to appear occupied," he said in his monotonic tone.

"Adopt a cube? What's this, the Humane Society?" I whispered to another engineer.

"Not really, there are no choices... all the adoptees are gray," he responded.

Engineers are a bowlful of laughs.

I was going to use my adoptee as a storage cube, which I thought was a great idea. I hoped no one else thought of that... but everyone did.

Many swapped their worn chairs with newer ones from the unoccupied cubes. Then everyone raced to fill their empty cube with old file drawer cabinets and stacks of three-inch binders. It was like Black Friday at Walmart without the elbowing.

Cube farm inhabitants...

I think I'm going to enjoy this section.

One was Bill—an engineer who smoked his glasses.

One day on my way to the lab, I glanced into Bill's cube to see him looking into the distance, holding readers in his right hand. The piece that hooks your ear was in his mouth, he was making soft puffing sounds, as if he were smoking a cigar.

"How are you doing, Bill?"

Bill didn't remove his glasses from his mouth. "Hi Glenn, just thinking about the design review next week." The glasses were like his pipe, occasionally clicking them on his teeth.

He had the doughy face of Roy Clark—the banjo-playing host of the TV series *Hee Haw*. (The TV program that aired from 1969 through 1997.) With his banjo, Roy was a pickin' and a grinin' whereas with his glasses, Bill was a puffin' and clickin'.

Ugh.

Okay, that was a groaner.

Another cube farmer was James. He was the first person I met who had a hyphenated last name. His was Culberson-Williamson. Sort of singsong. Did he search for a girl to marry with a last name that would rhyme with his?

No that couldn't be it.

Probably not. At work, many times people addressed you by your last name, and his was a mouthful, but he insisted that we use it.

"Hey, Culberson-Williamson, how's it going?"

Every time I said it, I felt like my mouth was full of food.

Yep, we grew tired of that, and someone labeled him the *hyphenator*.

He liked it, said he felt more part of the team. I guess you could think of the nickname as a term of endearment.

"Hey, hyphenator, how's it going?"

"Great! How 'bout you?"

James was a young likeable engineer but a bit goofy: he had unkempt hair, wore shirts that looked like he slept in them, and liked to keep odd hours—taking off during the day and staying into the night. Those were prehistoric times, long before flextime or working at home was a thing.

After three years, he resigned from the company for a better job. I was sorry to see him go. He celebrated his departure by throwing a party at his place—an old farmhouse, north of the plant on Third Street. He was heading to California to join up with his college friend. They had invented the software and electronics used in the *Tickle-me Elmo* toy. He was one of the *famous* engineers raised in our cube farm.

We also had our share of engineers from the farm on the local, national and international music scene. There probably were more musicians than the three I personally knew.

Try to keep it brief... although this could be interesting.
I'll try.

John was a quality engineer and played a mean sax in the St. Charles Municipal Band. They played big-band-type music, popular music and Latin music. John was a member of my Heads-up Display (HUD) product team. He was a huge and quiet guy, who was proud of his nickname given to him by the Japanese (the licensee for the HUD). It was *Zo*, which means elephant.

Jimmy was an electrical draftsman and the bass guitarist in Chuck Berry's band for over forty years. He played locally and traveled the country and the world with Chuck. Most of the band's tours were in the summer, so Jimmy used his vacation. His time off work was never questioned because he always completed his job on time. Anyway, Jimmy's story of his first guitar was legendary—he found a Harmony guitar with a broken neck in his step-father's barn, but with glue and new strings, he said it played like a Gibson. By the way, in 2018 Jimmy published a book, *Memories of Chuck*, about his times with Chuck Berry. I bought it on Amazon.

Homer was an electrical engineer and a member of the Dillard Brothers, an American Bluegrass band that became nationally popular for their appearance as *The Darlings* on the TV program *The Andy Griffith Show*.

On a side note: It was through Homer that I shook hands with a Monkee.

Huh?

The Monkees—Micky Dolenz, Michael Nesmith, Peter Tork and Davy Jones—were an American rock and pop band. The group was conceived in 1965 by television producers specifically for the situation comedy series that aired from 1966 to 1968. To their fans' delight, the band continued making hit songs long after the TV show was canceled.

That was before my time.

Anyway, Homer knew Micky Dolenz through the Dillard Brothers. Micky was interested in our company's sound systems, holograms and other electronic specialties that could be useful to musicians. During his tour of our company, I gave Micky Dolenz a demonstration of the Head up Display system, but he did not reciprocate by belting out a few notes of *Last Train to Clarksville*. To be fair, I didn't ask.

I loved those stories. I wish there were more than the three.

Wait. While I was writing about the demonstration, I remembered something about the HUD test set. I thought I'd put it here, even though it doesn't quite fit, but I didn't want to lose the thought.

Alright already... just tell me.

Okay. I asked the manufacturing test engineer to program Pong—the groundbreaking video game released in 1972 by Atari—into the test set. He did, and even though the display screen was small, playing Pong was so much fun for the HUD team, and for the crowds it drew during lunchtime and after working hours.

Oh, one final thing before I leave the cube farm… Miss Three-thirty

Who?

She wasn't a member of the engineering cube farm, but impacted our workday. The standard starting time and quitting time of the hourly employees and the salaried employees were staggered—seven to three-thirty and eight to four-thirty, respectively—to prevent traffic jams.

Anyway, she was a secretary in the manufacturing cube farm on the mezzanine overlooking the production floor—a blonde with a sweet face, a tight top, and a mini-skirt. Around manufacturing quitting time each day, she'd walk the entire length of the production area, heading to the back parking lot—heels clicking on the concrete floor, a sashay now and then, and eyes straight ahead. Many engineers found a reason to be on the production floor near the manufacturing quitting time. She knew everyone was watching her and made the most of it. The production workers, both men and women, would stop and gawk. She was *Miss Three-thirty*.

CARPOOLING

Don't remind me of that.

Carpooling is the art of ride sharing that can be a logistic nightmare.

It has been around since the beginning of time. From the prehistoric days, when the dinosaurs roamed the earth, Fred and Barney rode together to work at the Slate Rock and Gravel Company, to today, in the twenty-first century, carpooling is a daily event. Parents share the duties of hauling kids to school, sporting events and wherever, which sounds like a huge coordination effort to me. The carpool is part of our culture, a fixture in many of our daily lives, the very fiber of being human. It…

Wait! The fiber of being human?

Okay, I got carried away. It won't happen again.

Yeah, right.

I'm sure everybody remembers his or her first carpool, first teacher, first kiss, the first time… I think I'll stop there.

Carpools were encouraged at work, and the HR guys posted cutesy sayings on the bulletin boards like *East or West—carpooling is the best* and *Cut the fuel—carpool.*

My first carpool was with Len, a fellow electronic engineer. Each morning I'd drive from my home on Alaska Avenue, and he'd drive from his home on South Jefferson Avenue. We'd meet at a Kroger parking lot then head off to McDonnell Aircraft Company. In the 1960s, there was no concern about leaving your car in a grocery store lot in the Southside of St. Louis—car thefts happened, but were not a *thing* back then.

Len and I met through mutual friends, hit it off, became close workmates and close friends, and socialized through the years. However, punctuality was not his strong suit. I was on time, usually early, he was late, but somehow we made it to work on time every day. Our car conversations mainly covered St. Louis sports teams—Cardinal's Baseball, Cardinal's Football and Hawk's Basketball. I totally enjoyed those rides to work.

Len was an excellent engineer, sought after to be a member of everyone's project team, but his low priority for punctuality garnered him a dubious honor.

At work when an engineer would say, "Let's meet in five minutes to discuss the design."

Another engineer would invariably ask, "It that a Leonard-Five or an actual five."

You engineers were so funny.

Over the years, Len and I moved onto different projects, different carpools, and rarely saw each outside of work. When our paths did cross at work, we shared a coffee and talked about the old days. I always enjoyed his company, and we remained friends throughout our working careers. Sadly, Len died in 2004 at the age of sixty-five. At the funeral parlor, his wife, Jeanne, and I reminisced about our social times together and about Len and the carpooling days.

My second carpooling experience was a four-way. My car mates were Boyd, Fred, and Roger—BFR, if you're into acronyms. Boyd was a safety engineer, Fred was a mechanical engineer, and Roger, whom you met in an earlier chapter, was an electrical engineer. You'd think the conversation would be technically stimulating. What's your next guess?

Let's just keep it moving.

The driver of the day would pick up the others at their homes. We lived close to each other—it was a carpool of convenience. During the ride, Boyd would read the latest information on safety—boring, Fred would sleep as soon as he hit the seat—a guilt-free mind, and Roger would complain about work, weather, and politics. I'd zone out (not while I was driving), trying to remember that I was doing this to save money and help the environment.

As projects became more diverse and more demanding, everyone seemed to want to drive alone. Start early, stay late was the new mantra. Almost overnight, carpooling to and from work went from an in-thing to a dinosaur-thing.

QUALIFICATION TESTS AND THOSE WHO LOVED THEM

What are qualification tests?

From the way you asked that question, I sensed a *who-cares* attitude. Your tone seemed to say that you could certainly live without the answer. But the answer is exciting—it's verifying the integrity of the equipment. It's the electronic design versus the environment!

Sounds boring.

Even in dinosaur times, testing was a part of business life, a bit prehistoric and more dangerous but still a thing. For example, Fred Flintstone rode a brontosaurus as a crane operator for the gravel company. His seat was uncomfortable and not that sturdy, so he invented a new seat, which had to be tested. His brontosaurus wasn't thrilled about the test, but Fred prevailed. When Fred's new seat was adopted by other crane operators, his boss presented him with a certificate, which Fred proudly hung in his cave.

That was a fun example.

Thanks… but let's dive into testing.

Our customer required that electronic equipment pass a standard group of environmental tests before it can be certified for mass production. That testing was a huge part of product development at all engineering companies, including ours.

Qualification testing of *black boxes*—the cool name

for electronic equipment in the engineering industry—was the responsibility of Larry, our environmental engineer, and his team. Larry was old school. His testing sequences met military requirements, but his methods were improvised and unorthodox. He was an excellent engineer and a go-to resource in the field of *shake and bake* testing. Every time I use that phrase, I think the movie *Talladega Nights* with Will Farrell and John Reilly and their shake-and-bake routine at NASCAR events. If you haven't seen the film, get the DVD or stream it. The movie is crazy funny.

Anyway, qualification tests for cockpit equipment were routine until the addition of two new environments—*rain and chicken blood.*

I know what you're thinking, but let me assure you that we didn't wait for a rainy day to perform the rain test, and no chickens were injured or killed to perform the chicken-blood test. Those tests were developed because of two incidents.

Number one: The military noted that some aircraft parked on the runway had their cockpit canopies open. So they added some rain tests—they specified the exact nature of the testing—blowing rain, dripping water, and water ingress. Blowing rain tests specify wind velocity and rainfall rate, drip tests specify raindrop falling rate, and water ingress tests determine the effectiveness of seals on the equipment. Military specifications were very detailed.

Number two: Brothers Daniel and Philip Berrigan were American priests, anti-war activists, pacifists, playwrights, poets, and authors. Daniel landed on the FBI's most wanted list—the first-ever priest on the list—was featured on the cover of Time magazine, and spent time in jail. Philip married a former nun, and during eleven years of their twenty-nine-year marriage, one or both served time in prison.

Where's this going?

Hold on. You sound like one of those who crave instant gratification.

Anyway, at an anti-war protest, during a show and tell of military planes on the McDonnell Douglas airfield, the Berrigan Brothers pushed through a barrier, rushed toward an F-15 fighter aircraft, and threw bags of chicken blood into the open cockpit—causing the paint on the equipment to become discolored. Hence, the chicken-blood test was born.

Back to Larry, the environmental engineer. These new tests excited him. He was always up for a challenge.

The first step of the rain tests was to barricade the men's room.

What?

That's exactly what I thought. Where would we… wait! He's not going have us take a leak on the equipment. Is he? That would have been disgusting and ridiculous, but innovative. Don't worry, it didn't happen; it was only a wild rumor.

The barricade of the bathroom was greatly overblown; Larry attached an out-of-order sign to the door. He was a minimalist.

About a week later, the men's room looked like a *moonshiner's still*—hoses, meters, and barrels, all jury-rigged together, looking as if the whole contraption could topple at any minute.

Larry and his trusted sidekick, Charlie, explained at a peer review—an evaluation of scientific, academic, or professional work by others in the same field—the testing method and the sequence. In reality, the review was a bunch of engineers sitting around drinking coffee, talking Cardinal baseball, and nodding as the presenter droned on. Surprise, surprise. Larry's test method received the peer-review approval.

Monday morning at 9 a.m., I walked into the rain-testing lab (the men's room) and thought I was on the set of *The Andromeda Strain*—a movie about a virus gone wild. Larry and Charley were in thrift-shop hazmat suits.

"What are you guys doing? I don't recall that getup discussed in your presentation."

"There's going be a lot of spraying water," Larry said, as if he were the operator of the Log Flume ride at Six-Flags. "We don't want to eat lunch in wet clothes."

That sounded reasonable to me but a bit over the top. Then I recalled past Christmas seasons at the electronics company. Larry had programmed the vibration apparatus, which was used for black-box shake testing, to simulate Christmas music. Everyone's favorite was *White Christmas*. The notes from the vibration equipment barely suggested the tune, but when the engineers belted out—*I'm dreaming of a White Christmas*—the notes were truly melodious. I loved those times, felt like I was in a choir and connected to my fellow singers.

Anyway, back to rain testing. Excitedly, I stepped into the lab a few times to check on their progress, but there was more adjusting the measuring equipment than spraying water. The official testing only took a few hours, and the faux-hazmat suits seemed to be for show only.

The next week, I monitored the chicken-blood tests and expected hazmat suits might be appropriate this time around. But when I walked into the testing lab (again the men's room), I thought I was interrupting a round of Corn Hole—a lawn game in which players take turns throwing beanbags at a raised platform with a hole in its far end.

Are you going to define everything?

Sorry, just trying to be clear.

A mockup of a cockpit instrumental panel, coated with the new military-specified, chicken-blood resistant paint, sat in one of the urinals. Larry was tossing a bag of water at the panel.

"You have got to be kidding!" I said.

"This is the real deal," Larry answered. "I'm just practicing my arm movement and setting the throwing distance. Don't want to waste any military-approved bags filled with... the red *goo*. Care to toss one?"

Weeks later, our customer approved Larry's test report and certified that our equipment passed the rain and the chicken-blood tests. Another outstanding job by Larry and his environmental-testing team. He always came through, just like the post office—deliveries through rain, sleet and snow.

Really. The post office is a poor comparison.

Anyway, if you thought those testing setups were ingenious, Larry really shined during the Great Flood of 1993.

I was the project leader on a black box that was in the midst of qualification testing when the flood became a concern. Rivers and creeks were overflowing their banks—water, water everywhere and not a drop to drink. According to the National Weather Service flood predictions, our building would not be compromised but would be an island in three days.

"Our customer called, asking how the flood will impact the qualification testing." I told my project team, gathered at a morning meeting. "Larry, what's your guess on a schedule delay?"

"My friend has a boat," All heads turned to Al, a member of Larry's team. Al continued, "Larry and I talked about the flood and believe that we can continue the testing without interruption."

They wouldn't let a little water stop the qualification testing. It was the Conductron Navy to the rescue.

Wait! The Conductron Navy?

Yep. Our company's name was Conductron, and the navy was a fleet of one rowboat and two seamen.

Larry and Al made all the preparations, and the night before the launch, the project team had few beers at *Noah's Ark*—a local gathering place in St. Charles for after-work fun. (Sadly, the Ark fell out of favor and met its fate in 2007—a demolition crew leveled it to the ground. Now that location is The Streets of St. Charles.)

Wow, you snuck in that bit of trivia.

The day of the launch, the navy crew, another engineer and I stood on Third Street, watching the floodwaters lap against Building 500. The weather service called it correctly—the building was an island. I snapped a few pictures, then we pushed the boat into the muddy water. Larry and Al rowed, rowed, rowed, and rowed their boat through the Missouri River floodwaters to the back door of Building 500.

It was a successful mission—the qualification testing completed on time.

For you flood buffs...

Huh? I've heard of movie buffs, but I don't think a flood buff is a thing.

Anyway, on August 1, 1993, the Mississippi River at St. Louis crested at 49.58 feet, the highest stage ever recorded.

LET'S GO A SOLDERING

That title sounds eerily like the song "Let's go a wassailing."
It does... and since you brought it up...
Oh, no. I know what's coming. Why didn't I keep my mouth shut?
Wassailing is a very ancient custom, probably not practiced in dinosaur times, but who knows. Theories are that cavemen did their share of imbibing. Anyway, the legend about how wassailing became a thing says that a beautiful Saxon maiden named Rowena presented the handsome Prince Vortigen with a bowl of wine while toasting him—good health. Over the years, the wine morphed into wassail—a drink made of mulled ale, curdled cream, roasted apples, eggs, cloves, ginger, nutmeg and sugar.
That was a bit much, but interesting. Probably more interesting than soldering.
Just wait.
At my company, as at all hi-tech companies, there was an engineering lab where product designs were built (parts soldered on printed-circuit boards) and tested and was manned by technicians. The techs ordered parts from the engineering drawings, received and stocked them along with standard lab parts, and built and tested prototypes of an engineering design. Our crew of techs included Roger, whose nickname was *Niner* because of an unfortunate

accident at Home Depot; Dickey, who could imitate any sound and impersonate most celebrities of the time; and lastly, Bill and Palmer—the steadying forces of the crew. By the way, Palmer's first name was Glen—note that his had only one N, but I didn't hold that against him. The engineering lab was a gathering place, not only to build and test engineering designs, but also to have a coffee, exchange company gossip and share some laughs.

Anyway, Palmer taught me the art of soldering electronic parts to a printed-circuit board. There were no YouTube videos to walk you through the process. I learned the dinosaur way—from another person in the same room at the same workbench.

First of all, let's look what's involved in soldering—defining terms is an engineer's lifeblood. Soldering is the joining of metals by melting a filler metal into the joint. You need four items: a soldering iron—it plugs into a wall socket—a roll of solder, similar to a spool of thread, a tub of flux paste, and a muffin fan to blow soldering fumes away.

Wait! Muffin fan?

That's the name. So glad you asked. It's a small, usually five inches square, non-oscillating, high-airflow fan that moves the fumes away from the soldering process. If you want more details, check out the fans on Amazon.

Now the basics…

Number one: Solder is metal glue. Unlike in welding, only the filler metal, the solder, melts. The metals being joined usually have a much higher melting point than the solder. Brazing is another technique. It is similar to soldering in this regard; even though the filler metal in brazing melts at a much higher temperature than solder, the joined metals still don't melt.

Number two: Flux is the key. (Not the flux capacitor in the *Back to the Future* film series.) Flux has the ability to fight the mortal enemy of solder: metal oxides. Metal oxides prevent good solder joints because solder will not adequately adhere to a joint when there's a metal oxide coating. Flux is designed to remove metal oxides, and to do so while the joint is being soldered. Pre-cleaning the metals doesn't cut it, by the time the solder flows, atmospheric oxygen has rebuilt the metal oxide layer enough to spoil the soldering.

Oops, I think I went a bit too heavy on the technical details.

Ya think?

Even though soldering was the technicians' job, engineers still wanted to dabble. I wanted to solder to feel that I was a bigger part in building of the final product. I was excited to try. Palmer was an excellent and patient tutor, but as you may have guessed—my soldering techniques didn't pass muster. Although, I did master two of the common mistakes in soldering—I didn't burn my fingers after a few tries, and my hands became steadier, thus there were no disturbed joints. But to my regret, some of the joints were solder-starved, others formed a river of solder, and some were cold joints. And no, I'm not going to define cold joints.

Hurrah!

I know soldering is a dull topic to many, so I thought I'd end this chapter on a bright note. I mean a song. Enjoy!

Here we come a wassailing
Among the leaves so green,
Here we come a wassailing,
So fair to be seen:
Love and joy come to you,

And to you your wassail too,
And God bless you and send you,
A happy New Year,
And God send you,
A happy New Year.

SIX SIGMA

Oh no, this sounds like math.

The memo's title was *The Malcom Baldrige Quality Award.*

My first reaction was—Huh? Surely, I received this memo by mistake. Then I rechecked the addressees. Yep, my name was there. The memo's bottom line was—the electronics company was going to apply for the National Quality Award next year.

The first thing I did was check out *Dilbert*; the comic strip was always relevant. "In the olden days, quality meant good," Dilbert began. "Today, it has evolved into a complicated method for transferring your money to business consultants."

Dilbert nailed it. You'll understand his remarks as you read on.

The first meeting was an all-company meeting, a *Rah! Rah! Rah! Sis! Boom! Bah!* Message—quality will be part of your job.

Our quality czar said, "You will embrace quality. Quality is your friend…" I almost barfed. "…We've hired a quality consultant who will lead us to the award. It's going to be great."

Yeah, right. Who was he kidding?

At the second meeting, the consultant introduced himself as Johnathan Michael Logan, and made it perfectly clear it was Johnathan, not Jon, not Mike, not Logan.

"Hey, Johnny boy, what's up?" whispered the engineer sitting next to me.

I cleared my throat, trying to hold back a laugh. Engineers were not into formality.

Johnathan handed out three thick books, each eight-and-a-half by eleven paperbacks and each written by a quality guru. He spoke about the authors as if they were gods—gods of quality. They were William Edwards Deming—the high prophet of Quality, Joseph Moses Juran –the father of Quality Control, and Philip Bayard Crosby—the father of Quality Management. Note that they all used three names with an odd middle name, so they must be really important. I'm not making up those titles—Google them yourself.

I plan not to.

He also talked about other quality celebrities and their connection to the quality gods—so boring. One thing good about the meeting was he did not hand out a genealogical tree. That would've been weird. The bespectacled, trim, slightly balding Johnathan spoke as if he were a quality groupie, and his presentation was like *Downton Abbey Season 6*—lavish but a yawner.

I thought this exercise was just another HR wild scheme. I was wrong. The company went all in—from setting up a just-in-time procurement-manufacturing team to hiring a change agent. Was a change-agent a thing? I wondered. Turned out it was, and still is. He was a promoter, a silver-tongued seller of snake oil, helping us to embrace change, making change our friend, inserting change into our everyday thoughts. He made some good points, but overall it was a crock.

Anyway, the electronics company was all-hands-on-deck for the quality award, and the consultant's plan included a Q-engineer—his cutesy term for a quality engineer—assigned to every project. The Q-engineer allocated to my group was Paul, a good guy, a team player.

"We need our own *quality* poster boy," I said at our first team meeting after the big announcement. After the jokes and bawdy remarks faded, we unanimously landed on our guy: James Joseph Brown—the godfather of Soul. Note he had three names like the quality gurus. We broke into our song to seal the deal.

"Whoa! I feel good. I knew that I would, now. Yeah, I feel good. So good, so good, I got Q."

Really? I got Q.

Corny, but… moving on. As in any technical or business field, new acronyms and terms were part of the quality movement. No, I'm going to bore you with all of them… but how about two.

How about none?

Really? Okay, I'll do one.

The word is *Lean*. It was not a descriptive word for a body type or a cut of meat, or a diet fad advertisement. It was *lean operations*—a means of running an organization that focuses on providing greater customer satisfaction while using as few resources as possible. Fewer resources? That sounded like layoffs to us engineers.

Anyway, *lean* became part of our everyday conversations: at our lunchtime card game—deal me some lean cards; at the hop—he's a lean mean dancing machine; at break time—I gotta take a lean.

That was childish.

Now… here's what you've been waiting for—Six Sigma, the name of the chapter. Six Sigma (6σ) is a set of techniques and tools for process improvement.

History alert! Bill Smith, an engineer at Motorola, coined the term Six Sigma in 1980. Then it got wildly popular when Jack Welch, the CEO of General Electric, made it central to his business strategy in 1995.

Thanks for the warning, but it didn't make the blurb interesting.

Anyway, our quality consultant, Johnathan, was passionate about Six Sigma. He ended his speech with the statistic, "The Six Sigma process yields 99.99966 % of all opportunities to produce some feature of a part to be free of defects." His face moved into something that looked like a smile, but I wasn't sure. Then, "That number is better than Proctor and Gamble's ad—Ivory Soap is 99 and 44/100% pure. Who would have guessed?"

I don't get the Ivory Soap thing.

I figured that readers under a certain age would not get that reference, but... go with it.

Anyway, I saw eyes rolling, mine included, and heard whispers of *who cares* rippling through the audience. Johnathan never knew when to stop.

As it turned out, we didn't win the Quality Award in 1993. We lost to Eastman Chemical Company and Acme Rubber Corporation—both are still in business, the electronics company is not. I don't think there's any conclusion to be drawn, just a coincidence. Our effort to win the award was not lost—the Boeing Tanker and Airlift Program based their submission on our work and won the award in 1998.

One more thing.

An overheard conversation...

"Cheryl, schedule a staff meeting," a department head asked his secretary.

"What's the topic?" Cheryl's pencil was poised over her notebook.

"I plan to fuse Six Sigma with lean methods to eliminate the gap between our strategies and our objectives."

"I'll just say waste of time."

BOWLING AT THE CORNER BAR

Isn't a bar for drinking?

Yep, and there was more beer drinking than bowling at the Corner Bar.

During my years at the electronics company in Building 500, I occasionally joined some engineers for an after-work beer and a few games of bowling. It was cocked-hat bowling... but more on that later.

First a bit of history: At over one hundred and fifty years old, the Corner Bar is the oldest bar in St. Charles and the second-oldest in Missouri. It was originally constructed in 1860 as part of a military school—the bottom floor built as stables, the first and second floors for classrooms and dormitories. When the Civil War ended, the building became a saloon, with the bowling lanes added in the basement around 1875.

Very interesting, but I already forgot most of those facts.

No worries, there is no quiz. The bar stands—more correctly leans toward the Missouri River—on the corner of First Capitol and Sixth Street. Get it? Corner Bar. Corner. Well, you probably already suspected that.

Anyway, the first time I descended the dimly-lit narrow steps to basement, it reminded me of the stairs to a dungeon—worn handrails, creaky wooden steps and a dank smell. At the bottom of the stairs was a yellow wooden fence, beyond that were a pair of bowling lanes underneath two stone archways, not a décor that screams—let's have fun. But as you can guess, beer and bowling go hand-in-hand and always deliver an entertaining time.

I know you are anxiously awaiting to learn about the term cocked-hat bowling.

I'm on the edge of my seat.

Well, cocked-hat bowling, originated in a pub in England and is played with three pins on narrower and shorter lanes than a standard tenpin bowling alley. The balls are only five inches in diameter and have no finger holes. The game got its name from the way bowlers used to wear their hats when playing—a bit cocked.

That was not worth the wait.

Anyway, at the Corner Bar lanes, everything was manual—keeping score on a chalk board, climbing the stairs for another round of beer, and a fast-moving teenaged pinsetter. (It reminded me of my grade-school days as a pinsetter at St. Anthony's Bowling Alley.)

Games had four bowlers at a time, two for each lane, I was paired with Joel, my Bridge partner, against... I can't recall their names, but we usually won. No memorable games—it was always fast rolling balls, lots of guy talk and cold draft beer. Nearly one hundred and fifty years later, the lanes are still there. Talk about a dinosaur that survived.

By the way, the Corner Bar is a popular place. The advertisement is minimal—a chalk board on the sidewalk, noting the day's lunch special, and word of mouth about its friendly pub atmosphere.

I still go to the Corner Bar once a month to have lunch and drinks with former Building 500 employees. It is a fun time, and I look forward to those monthly Wednesdays...

and you guessed it—we have prehistoric conversations.

Now, reminiscing about my times at the bar reminds me of the Mary Hopkin's 1968 anthem—*Those Were the Days*. Some of the lyrics are:

Those were the days my friend
We thought they'd never end
We'd sing and dance forever and a day
We'd live the life we choose
We'd fight and never lose
For we were young and sure to have our way

If you never heard of that song, check it out on YouTube.

IMMERSION

Is he talking about baptism?

No. In preparation for my time in Japan, I attended...

Wait! I did tell you about Japan, didn't I? Now I'm not sure. I could page through the previous chapters to verify that or just... Okay, here's the story.

In the 1980s, Japan received a license to produce the F-15 Fighter Aircraft, including its electronic systems. One of those systems was the Head up Display (HUD), which I had the responsibility for its design and production. Included in the license was the requirement to perform *qualification tests* on the *black boxes* of the systems in Japan. Good thing you remember those technical terms, otherwise I'd have to define them.

I don't remember, but thank you so much for not defining them again.

Shimadzu Electric, the Japanese company that was licensed to build the HUD, sent engineers to the electronics company to learn the design and the manufacturing process. In preparation for the Japanese visit and my impending trip to Japan, I was selected to learn Japanese. My youthful exuberance told me— Japanese class was going to be exciting.

I attended the Berlitz School of Language to learn conversational Japanese; the sessions were on Tuesday and Thursdays for three months. I took the classes with

John, a manufacturing engineer, whom I worked with on the Head up Display. He had the assignment to be our resident technical representative in Japan for a year.

The school was in an office building in Clayton, Missouri, and my instructor was Seiko Tanamachi. I can use her real name because I'm friends with her on Facebook. After introductions and some American humor—she smiled politely when John and I laughed—she escorted us to the classroom. Think about an interrogation room you've see on TV police shows, but a less harsh color and more comfortable chairs.

In her sweet, soft voice, Seiko said in perfect English, "Here at Berlitz, we use the immersion method to teach languages." John and I glanced at each other. Then she said, "After today, we will only speak Japanese in this room."

My lungs constricted. Beads of sweat formed on my forehead. No English? Was that even humane?

"Let's start with Japanese greetings." She pronounced each word distinctly. She spoke better English than I did. "In Japan, as in most countries, the greeting depends on the time of day—one for the morning, one for the afternoon and another for the evening."

I nodded, terrified like a Kindergarten student on the first day of school.

"Ohayo gozaimasu," she said with twinkling eyes and slight smile.

John and I stumbled over each syllable, and to her, we probably sounded, as if we were babies learning to speak. Our words were unrecognizable. Her ears were probably in pain, but she still smiled.

Then she spoke each syllable. "Ohio... goes... eye... moss."

I repeated the syllables, each time a bit faster, then faster yet, until finally, "Ohayo gozaimasu." Holy shit! I was speaking Japanese. I loved the immersion method. It's going to be great... but you guessed it—my euphoria was short-lived.

Next, was the afternoon or have-a-good-day greeting— *konnichiwa*, then the good evening greeting—*konbanwa*.

I faltered over the new Japanese words, struggling over each syllable, and sweating more profusely, then mercifully, the forty-five minute, first class ended.

"I will see you on Thursday," Seiko said.

Were those the last English words I would hear in the inquisition room? Maybe not. Maybe she'll feel sorry for us. She didn't. The only English words she spoke was when she introduced new Japanese words and phrases.

The classes were arduous. My brain was tired, and although I was only in my thirties, stumbling over pronunciations made me feel like a geezer.

I won't bore you with my struggles in learning the Japanese language.

Thank you so very much.

But one word caused a stir. That word was nightclub— the Japanese translation was *naito kurabu*.

I wondered why that word was important. What about library, museum, or gallery? I blurted, "Why is nightclub an important word?"

She was silent for a moment, ignoring my transgression into English, then said, "Nightclubs are popular in Japan. They're only for men, typically businessmen, who go there to drink, relax and to be served by Japanese women."

Wild thoughts swirled in my mind. What did served by Japanese women mean? Surely not... "Are the women Geishas?"

"Not Geishas. Geishas are Japanese women who entertain through performing the ancient traditions of art and dance, and wear kimonos and oshiroi makeup. In nightclubs, the Japanese women are hostesses, wearing street clothes, serving drinks and light snacks, and are there for conversation and to help the businessmen to unwind."

That sounds sexist.

Those words were my instructor's. It was the 1970s.

Anyway, the nightclub sounded like a place I'd like to go, (I did, but that story is for a future chapter.) and that brief conversation in English was a relaxing break. But I knew we'd go back to speaking Japanese, so I thanked her in Japanese. "Arigato."

She smiled, surely unimpressed and probably heard it a zillion times. "Nightclub is naito kurabu." She nodded— her indication for us to repeat the Japanese word.

I learned to speak and remember Japanese nouns quite well, putting them into sentences, not so much, other than the basics like asking someone's name, the time, directions, counting and speaking pleasantries like hello, thank-you, and excuse me.

Speaking of counting, one to ten in Japanese (ichi, ni, san, shi…) was easy to learn; however, the kicker was that a different modifier was added to each number depending on what you were counting—people, chairs animals. I thought—you've got to be kidding. I'd never say that aloud.

Anyway, the night before our last class, I thought about the Japanese nightclubs and figured I needed a sentence, an odd sentence, to show that I was trying to learn the language. Even today, I'm still not sure how I settled on my special sentence—the elephant has a red pencil.

The next day Seiko spoke English. "Since this is our last class..." she began. "...I thought if you have any questions, any requests, any phrases we didn't cover, I could help you now."

John shrugged, but I was ready. I had my question. "How do you say *the elephant has a red pencil*?" As soon as I said it, I realized that American humor was not humorous to the Japanese. But I didn't know it at the time that it was a good choice—the Japanese engineers, who were to visit the electronics company and would be with John and I in Japan, did develop a knack for enjoying American humor.

Seiko didn't speak for a moment, didn't lose her composure, didn't ask why that sentence, and didn't smile, she just answered it. I'd have been shocked if she acted any other way. She was Japanese. "Zō wa aka enpitsu imasu."

At the end of the last class, she handed us our certificates, then gave John and me a surprise—she invited us to share a traditional Japanese dinner at her and her husband's apartment on the Washington University campus.

John and I brought a bottle of sake, some St. Louis trinkets and a few company giveaways. She thanked us profusely—in English—as if our gifts were the best in the world. We took our shoes off at her door and followed her into an eating area—pillows scattered around a rectangular coffee table. The table was set with napkins, chopsticks and blue-and-white patterned dinner plates. During the evening, I threw in a few of my Japanese phrases, trying to show her that I had learned something, but Seiko didn't respond in kind; she wanted to speak English.

The evening was delightful, and it was obvious that

Seiko spent time preparing the delicious meal. Her husband arrived just as we were getting ready to leave. We said our goodbyes, and I never saw Seiko again.

THE NIGHTCLUB

I was hoping you'd tell us about it.

Kyoto, the cultural capital of Japan, is home to numerous temples, shrines, palaces and gardens. During my time in Japan, I cherished visiting all of those sites, but now they're mushed together in a blur. However, my evening at the nightclub is crystal clear.

Anyway, one afternoon at Shimadzu Electric Company in Kyoto, four Japanese engineers, John, and I were in a conference room. We were finishing a review of the qualification testing results of the day and the plans for the next day. (Those Japanese were the ones I had taught the theory of operation of the HUD System back in St. Charles, Missouri.)

A soft rap on the door interrupted the meeting.

Mr. Joh, the director of engineering, stepped into the room. "How is everything going?"

One of the Japanese engineers stood. "We just finished."

"Good, I'd like Roth san and Sartori san (That was John and I) and Nishi san (the most senior Japanese engineer at the table) to join me at Yokoso tonight." He bowed and left the room. He didn't wait for a response. We were going no matter what.

"What's Yokoso?" I asked Nishi.

"It's a popular night crub." (Japanese have difficulty pronouncing the letter L.) He paused for a moment, then added, "It means welcome."

My mind spun back to my Japanese classes and the word *nightclub*—the-for-men-only entertainment spots. Anticipation was mixed with a bit of nervousness.

Later that night, Mr. Joh and Nishi stopped by our hotel, and John and I joined them in a large cab. We were off to the nightclub. The cab driver wove through traffic, speeding through the Kiyamachi nightlife district of Kyoto, as if he were in a movie chase scene. He abruptly turned into a side street that looked like an alley—a dimly lit alley. He stopped at a narrow green door; the neon sign above it read *Yokoso*.

The Tony Orlando and Dawn's song lyrics—*better knock three times on the green door*—popped into my mind. In this situation, knocking wasn't necessary.

I stayed in my seat for a moment, forcing my tinge of motion sickness to abate, then hopped out of the cab and joined the others.

"Mr. Joh." A woman in a bright red, floral-patterned kimono met us at the door and bowed as she spoke. "We are so pleased that you could join us tonight." Gratitude and warmth covered her words like honey.

"Mama san," Mr. Joh replied, bowing as he spoke.

"Our ladies are waiting for you. Please follow me." Mama san said in a soft sweet voice.

Nishi bowed, indicating that John and I follow Mr. Joh. Our small parade walked single-file down a short hallway, Japanese art covering the walls, air bursting with incense, and into a room where four exquisite Japanese girls were all smiling, all beautiful, all wearing short skirts and loose fitting blouses. They bowed and indicated that we sit in a spacious, semi-circular booth. We slid into the booth in a boy-girl-boy-girl seating arrangement.

Sounds cozy to me.

Mama san and another Japanese woman filled our table with finger food—a bowl of seasoned peas, something that looked like hummus, oddly shaped crackers, a bowl of nuts, a plate of Shushi—and glasses of water around. Then Mama san said in the most pleasant voice I had ever heard, "What would you like?"

I was hoping she meant drinks.

"We will start with *biru*," Mr. Joh said. "Maybe Sapporo?"

Four bottles of beer came in an instant, as if the order was telepathically communicated to the bartender, or was Mr. Joh's standard order.

Before I could move, the girl next to me snatched my beer and poured the amber lager into a glass, so slowly it seemed that if she spilled a drop, she'd be reprimanded.

Mr. Joh lifted his glass in the air and looking at John and me, he said, "I am so happy that you could join me tonight. Kanpai!"

Moments later, the girl turned to me and with a slight head bow, said in nearly perfect English, "My name is Sachiko Hidari." Her face was more than blemish-free—it was pore-free. She showed no teeth when smiling, and I guessed her to be in her early twenties.

I nodded. "My name is Glenn Sartori." Why was I sweating? This was going to be a fun night.

"Ah so… *Gren Satori*. Nice to meet you."

We stumbled through an awkward conversation, too boring to relate here, but when I reached for my beer, she beat me to it again. Was she going hold the glass as I drank? No. She wiped the bottom of the glass with a napkin, so that no condensation would drip on my pants, and handed the glass to me.

Wow! Talk about service.

The beers were followed by another round and a refill of the finger-food. Everything was going fine until I excused myself to go the bathroom—my girl, Sachiko, followed me. Uh, oh. My Japanese classes hadn't prepared me for this. What was going to happen? Would she follow me into the bathroom? I knew Japanese had a less puritanical view of that than Americans did.

A few days before, John and I had taken a road trip that ended in Nara—a former capital of Japan and famous for its tame deer ranging freely in the city. We bought some food and ate at a picnic bench in a park. And as advertised, deer roamed the area but were disinterested in our food. Before we left for the ride back, we headed for the park's bathroom, a wooden structure open on two sides, and followed men and women, no deer, into the building. You could take care of business in a trough filled with running water or in one of the many doorless stalls. A breath caught in my chest and an uneasiness filled by body. But no one seemed to mind, men lined up against the wall, women headed to stalls. As the proverb says—when in Rome, do as the Romans do. And I did.

Back to the nightclub, Sachiko followed me to the bathroom, wiped the door handle with a moist towelette, and to my relief, she did not follow me inside. When I came out she was standing there and handed me a fresh warm towelette. This place was first class

Next came a round of sake and sheets of paper with song titles—the call for karaoke.

I gulped. I wasn't going to do karaoke. I can't carry a tune in a bathtub.

"What are you going to sing, Sartori-san?" Mr. Joh asked.

Yep. I was going to do karaoke.

I looked at John. He shrugged and gave me the open palm move—you go ahead. What a friend. Although I would've done the same if he were chosen first. So, I leafed through the papers, searching for a song title that I could, sort of talk through, rather than sing. I settled on *I Left My Heart in San Francisco.*

"I love that song," Sachiko said gleefully. "I can't wait to hear you sing, Satori san." She sounded like a groupie.

My pits instantly dampened.

Long story short…

I hate that phrase.

When I finished, the table applauded. My face warmed—the adulation made me feel good, even though I knew it was obligatory.

After a few more rounds of drinks and karaoke—Mr. Joh was quite the singer—Mama san appeared at our table, and Mr. Joh said, "Thanks for a lovely evening."

No hugs but a lot of bowing.

Outside, our cab was waiting. Those two hours flew by, and our time at the nightclub was over. Mama san and Mr. Joh waved to us as the taxi pulled away. Was Mr. Joh staying for another round? Or something else? It was none of my business. He had paid for the evening.

People crowded the streets. Nightlife in Kyoto was in full swing. (The nightclubs of Japan did not go the way of the dinosaurs. They still perform the same services that I enjoyed in the 1980s, but now go by the name Hostess Clubs.)

"Nishi san," I said and bowed my head. "That was a fun time."

"I'm happy you enjoyed yourself, Sartori san."

A happy buzz engulfed me, and as soon as I blurted, "How much did that cost?" I realized that was rude.

93

Shamefully, I still wanted to know.

Nishi san looked up at the cab roof, probably converting yens to dollars or thinking—those Americans. Moments later, he said, "Around three thousand dollars."

SUPERVISORS—THE GOOD AND THE BAD

I can totally relate.

Yep, most people can. My first supervisor was an engineer. Made sense—I was an engineer, and likewise for the other disciplines: contract people reported to a contract person, financial people reported to a financial person, and…

Over my career, the engineering supervisors I had were good guys, common-sense guys and interested in developing an excellent product. I was lucky.

That supervisory structure worked great until the company went to a new reporting system—the *matrix*, not like the Keanu Reeves movie trilogy, which was really cool by the way. In the company's matrix, every engineer had two supervisors: one was your department head, the other was your program manager. What human resource person pulled that system out of his…

That's when I experienced the full spectrum of supervising styles—from one-of-the-guys to my-way-or-the-highway. Surprisingly, the matrix worked fine because each supervisor had different marching orders—department heads worked to improve the engineers' skills and their fit in the organization. Whereas, the program manager worked to meet the product schedules. That functioned until it was raise time. Each supervisor wanted his input to be the deciding factor on the dollar amount of the employee's raise—talk about an arm-twisting contest. By the way, I used *his* because during most of my years in the hi-tech industry, the glass ceiling was Plexiglas—nearly impenetrable.

That was fine, but when do we get to the good stuff?

Hold on… I thought that was good stuff, but how about the next stories.

First of all, some of my colleagues used the Dinosaur Strategy when dealing with supervisor directives. The strategy involved ignoring all new management dictates while lumbering along doing the same things the same way you had always done them. What made this strategy successful was that it usually took nearly a year before the supervisor noticed the rebellion. Coincidently, that's about the length of time any boss stayed in the job.

I think I might try that.

I wouldn't.

My department manager loved the *five-fifteen*—a weekly status report that theoretically takes fifteen minutes to write and five minutes to read. Yeah, right. In my reality, it took thirty minutes to write and one minute to read.

First thing Monday morning, the department manager had a stand-up meeting—you know… like we actually stood—which he thought was efficient. There were six reports, mine included. Each of us would read our five-fifteen to the total boredom of the others, who were all anxious to get back to work. But over time it became a painless exercise. As the dinosaurs, it became extinct and was replaced by a weekly sit-down meeting on Friday mornings, sort of a recap of the week and plans for the coming week. Still boring, but only longer.

One program manager was Larry, notorious for

his rough and insensitive method of dealing with his subordinates. He was like a Neanderthal, keeping people in line with a loud threatening tone. Larry was a big guy, sat like *Jabba the Hut* with a protruding gut and seemed proud of it. The shirt button above his belt was generally open, exposing—I'm not describing the view because you won't be able to unread it, so... just use your imagination.

Yuck!

On one occasion, Larry asked me to write a detailed report on the design status of my Guidance Interface Unit project. The GIU was a black box, part of the electronic suite in the Stand-Off Land Attack Missile (SLAM). I loved working on that project. It was challenging and rewarding.

On the day of the first test launch, the SLAM team stayed at work into the evening to hear the results of the missile test. The U.S. Navy was to conduct its first live fire of a SLAM from a fighter aircraft into a building complex test site on a remote island. About six of us huddled in the marketing guy's office, waiting for the call of a successful hit.

The missile was marketed for its surgical precision, and I was sure that it would do its thing. It did. I was elated. We cheered and clicked bottles. Oops. Don't tell anyone that we had some beers. And the next week, I was given a copy of the video tape that showed the SLAM entering the window of the building and moments later, a second missile hitting the exact same location.

That was awesome.

Back to Larry, I stepped into his office and handed him my report. "Here it is, Larry." I spoke with pride in my voice.

He read it, then "No, not this. Rework it."

Even though I heard that response before, I was devastated. Others had the same experience too. He was notorious for not telling what he wanted, maybe he didn't even know. But that's how he operated—you keep tweaking your report until he said it was good. This time I had a plan. I'd sit on it for a few days, reprint it with a new date, and resubmit without any changes. What's the worst that could happen? He could thump his shoe on his desk—an imitation of the shoe-banging incidents by Nikita Khrushchev. I had witnessed that in more than one meeting.

Two days later, "Here it is, Larry." I fought to keep an even tone as sweat seeped from my pits.

He read it, then, "Looks good. Let's go with it."

BUILDING 500

You have to be kidding. This chapter is about a building?

It was more than a building. It provided a workspace, of course, but also a friendship-forming, high-tech-designing, enjoyable environment. I spent over half of my career there and loved it. My time in Building 500 reminds me again of the Mary Hopkin anthem—*Those were the days my friends, we thought they'd never end. We'd...*

Anyway, on my daily trek to Building 500, I drove over the Missouri River on the dilapidated Rock Road Bridge, which connected St. Louis County to the City of St. Charles. The drive across the narrow, two-lane bridge was slow, scary. At its narrowest dogleg, motorists would scrape the rail, marking it with their car paint, or leave a door handle or side mirror, as a remembrance of their drive to work. Or was it the spooky bridge that attacked the car? Could be—the bridge opened in April of 1904, in time for the St. Louis World's Fair, so it was old and cranky.

After surviving the bridge ordeal, the drive was smooth sailing. I rolled through the old section of North St. Charles, appreciating the gothic buildings of the Academy of the Sacred Heart, the mom-and-pop businesses, and the popular A&W Root Beer joint, where carhops served you, and you ate in your car.

Did they wear roller skates?

No they didn't, but they did elsewhere as depicted in the movie classic *American Graffiti*.

Building 500 housed engineering, manufacturing, business offices and company leadership all under the same roof. At our peak, we were over a thousand employees, but less than a hundred at our demise, and I was there for it all. Womb to tomb as they say.

Now for some highlights of my life in Building 500.

Okay, I'm ready.

Our Presidents…

The building's leadership was a revolving door policy. The corporate bigwigs changed electronic company presidents every two to five years.

Why?

Well… we were a proving ground, a get-your-feet-wet company for those fair-haired, leaders not quite ready to take over huge operations. Those anointed ones followed our first president—Kip Siegel.

Keeve Milton (Kip to his friends) Siegel received his BS from Rensselaer Polytechnic Institute, hired by the University of Michigan in Ann Arbor as a professor of physics, and founded Conduction Corporation, which McDonnell Douglas absorbed into its operations and later became the Electronics Company. By the way, Kip has a Wikipedia page.

One afternoon, Kip announced an assembly of all employees, as if he were a high-school principal. I joined the crowd in the manufacturing area and listened to his plans that he voiced through a bullhorn—we are going to… *develop nuclear fusion as an energy source, sell our foliage penetration radar to the military, manufacture high-energy lasers, and put gas air conditioners in all homes.* He was passionate guy, but... Surprise! None of those came to fruition, although he air-conditioned the manufacturing area, probably because he was sweating profusely during his rah-rah speech.

After Kip's retirement, I witnessed a parade of presidents. Next was David Clem Arnold, who was around the longest, seemed to care, and definitely vested in the Japanese project that I led. At his home in Elsah, Illinois, on the bluffs overlooking the Missouri River, he hosted a farewell party for the visiting Japanese engineers. The evening was delightful. I had a great time, sharing stories of our times together in Building 500, and enjoying the abundance of food and drinks. Clem stayed in the St. Louis area after his retirement and sadly, died in 2011 at the age of 91.

Then, there were presidents John Wolf, followed by David Swain, both rumored to have ties to the McDonnell family (fairly typical in big corporations). Then a former pentagon director, Pete Aldridge, moved the headquarters to McLean, Virginia, and changed our name to McDonnell Douglas Electronics Systems Company.

Boy, that name slides off your tongue.

He fed us the line that the HQ should be near our customer—the military in DC. He didn't fool anybody—his family lived there—and brought in no new business as he promised.

Each revolving-door president had his own ideas how to reorg the business and most seemed not to give a shit, and never stuck around to see the results—maybe some wanted to, but the corporate ladder was beckoning. This frequent changing of the guard drove us quicker down the path to our demise.

Our Products...

Many of the electronic company products were ahead of their time. In the 1970s, we designed and marketed holographic images, so commonplace today that you can buy them on Amazon; laser discs—the forerunner of DVDs; the first Head up Display (HUD), now available in cars; (The HUD project was my favorite. I spent many years leading it, and it took me to Japan and on other international jaunts.) VITAL, the first visual flight simulator, now a product of Flight Systems Inc.; electronic speech generation and voice recognition systems, now everywhere today. Can you say Alexa? And there were many others. We developed and marketed too many hi-tech products, which contributed to our fall from grace.

Lunchtime Bridge...

I brown-bagged most days—time was of the essence, no time to go to the cafeteria. I was in a duplicate Bridge club, playing four hands during our thirty-minute lunch period.

Wow!

Yes, that was a fast pace. And we were bigtime—the American Contract Bridge League (ACBL) sanctioned our club and awarded master points, which were like the gold stars you earned in Kindergarten. I was proud of my thirty-four master points, which made me a club master. Not a big whoop, considering you needed 300 points to be a Life Master and 10,000 points plus a victory over another 10,000-point player to be a Grand Master.

That's more than I wanted to know.

You're right... I got a bit carried away. But Bridge is

the best game ever. It involves complex logical reasoning, probability, people-reading, deception, communication and coordinated action between teammates. I loved it—started playing in college, played in tournaments around the city, and even joined a Bridge club at church. The players in the church club began dying off, so my wife and I were one of the last pairs standing. Sadly, it is an old person's game, not an instant gratification game desired by today's youth.

You're still talking Bridge.

I don't play anymore, but I'm a Bridge dinosaur—I read the Bridge column in the daily newspaper and as dinosaurs do—belittle the bidding sequence and the off-the-wall play.

The Demolition...

The rickety St. Charles Rock Road Bridge closed on December 17, 1992, eighty-two years after it opened, and its demolition began soon after that. There was a small park behind Building 500, a great vantage point for watching the bridge destruction and the new construction up river. The demolition drew large crowds—people always love to see things blown up—and these explosions soon became events. Common sights were hotdogs grilling on the park's BBQ pits, people lounging in lawn chairs and throwing back a few cold ones. Luckily, this took place while I worked in Building 500. After the completion of the demolition, the crowd thinned, only a few bridge-buffs and McDonnell Douglas employees viewed the bridge replacement down river.

The End...

Our times in Building 500 could never be duplicated; they were unique, glorious and unrivaled. My group was the last in the building; everyone else had packed up and moved out. We needed to celebrate in some way. Food was brought in for lunch every day that final week, but for the last day, I organized a golf tournament ... inside the building.

That sounds cool.

It was. The well-worn carpet was like indoor Astro-Turf, which provided an adequate putting surface. We set up three holes by digging out pieces of the carpet, made score cards, and awarded trophies... even had a boisterous gallery, although drinking was prohibited on company property. The top golfers received a trophy, and their names were... I don't remember.

The end was a bittersweet time, but we knew that those years spent together couldn't just end. They didn't. The Building 500 family lived on through picnics and reunions.

I bet there is a chapter on picnics.

You're right. It's next.

THE PICNICS AKA REUNIONS

Who doesn't love a picnic? Even teddy bears love picnics.

They do, and I remember their song—if you go down in the woods today, you're sure of a big surprise. If you go…

Stop. I've heard it on You Tube… I think Ann Murray sang it.

Okay. How many people do you need for a picnic? Two people could be a picnic—throw a blanket on the ground, open a basket of wine, cheese and treats, and share some laughs and maybe some kisses. Or it could be the residents of a small town—who gather to celebrate a holiday, like the Fourth of July, play games, and eat and drink—most probably have less drama than in William Inge's 1953 Pulitzer Prize-winning play *Picnic*.

Maybe you remember a family picnic, school picnic or a company picnic.

No, I hate eating with insects.

Oh… But I'd like to tell you about our epic company picnics.

Epic?

The McDonnel Douglas Electronics Company had a Management Club, which organized six events a year—meetings with food, drinks and a notable speaker, an event with spouses, and a club picnic. When I was the president of the Management Club, I noticed that the picnic had the most attendees and brought about the most camaraderie among the members.

After the club disbanded—I think in the early 1980s—I talked with some of my engineering workmates about reviving the picnic, except make it companywide.

I think my idea found its way to upper management. Because in 1985, the electronic company's president, John Wolf, authorized our first and only open house and companywide picnic.

After that picnic, there was lots of talk but no action until the announcement that Building 500 was going to close. As the end approached, we all looked back on those times in Building 500 and realized that we had something special. The talk bubbled up about getting together for a picnic or something, something to keep us in contact. That talk led to action—we formed a picnic committee with a host of eager volunteers. Maggie, one of the secretaries, and I were the co-chairs of the committee. The first Building 500 Picnic took place in St. Charles in Blanchette Park in September of 1995.

Picnics—later labeled Reunions—were held every other year (the term is biennial for those interested) in the fall at Blanchette Park. The attendance count exploded as word traveled about how much fun the event was.

Over three hundred employees attended that first reunion in 1995, and over five hundred attended the fifth reunion in 2003, where people came from not only the St. Louis-St. Charles area, but from out-state Missouri, Illinois, Arkansas, Iowa, Colorado, Texas, Florida, Mississippi and California.

Really. Did you have to list all the states?

Some even had set their vacation plans around the reunion—that's quite a testimonial to the special relationships we had in Building 500.

As expected, there were start-up crinkles in the first picnic; the worst was—the beer was running low.

"Hey, Glenn…" a picnic goer called to me. "…we're almost out of beer."

"Beer run!" Somebody yelled and then his words turned into a chant as in the movie *Animal House*.

It was an obvious emergency.

I hopped into my car with a relatively sober guy and headed to the neighborhood IGA store. We filled a cart with cases of ice-cold beer, and when I plunked down a wad of bills, I received a leery glance from the checkout person. I just smiled. I didn't want to get into a conversation—picnic attendees were getting thirsty.

Catastrophe avoided. However, we had purchased too much, which, as you might have guessed, the few remaining drinkers couldn't let those cold ones go to waste. That first picnic disbanded after one in the morning. How some of those guys got safely home still amazes me. We should have taken their keys, offered to drive them home, or called an Uber… wait a minute, there was no such thing back then.

While planning the sixth picnic—the date of this event was October 6, 2005—I realized that I just wanted to be a picnic attendee, and spend the time socializing, not responsible for working for its success. Maggie felt the same. We recruited Sharon, an eager and well-liked employee. She carried on the tradition with a great spirit and new ideas. She had the picnic totally catered, reducing the number of volunteers, which Maggie and I had always struggled to recruit.

Sharon and her committee carried the torch for the next six picnics, the last one was in September 2017.

With the crowd dwindling (a natural outcome, since the picnic goers were only workers of the non-existent Building 500), Sharon wanted to pass the torch, but no one stepped up to take her place, so... sadly the picnics are now only happy memories.

I loved those reunions, and I know all the attendees did, too. Looking back over the picnics that spanned twenty-two years, things changed dramatically. The early picnics ended near midnight, most recent ones had the crowd starting to leave around nine; in the first few picnics, we drank lots of beer—had to make to some beer runs—later picnics, more bottled water was drunk than beer; and at the end, nearly all the picnic goers were retirees, yet camaraderie always filled the air at every picnic. It was special. It was epic.

Okay. I have to give you that the picnics were one of a kind.

Thanks. They certainly were. Even though the picnics are no more, I still have fond memories of those times, the exciting programs I worked on, and the people that I worked with in Building 500.

TRAVELING FOR THE MAN

Oh, no. Boring travel stories. I'm definitely skipping this chapter.

Wait! This is not like... your friends inviting you over for dinner, only to subject you to a slide show—oops, that technology was popular in prehistoric times—or a video of their latest jaunt to an exotic place.

This chapter is not like that? How so?

Think of it this way. No matter the length—days or weeks—or he destination—national or international—traveling turns everyone into a storyteller.

Oh. You're right. I've done that.

You're still reading... great. I hadn't planned to insert a chapter about my company trips, but one of my readers told me that it might be entertaining... only if it's brief.

I love brevity. Less is more.

Oh, now my reader is a philosopher. Nevertheless, the thought of business trips for my company excited me—see world sights on the company's dime, or in present day lingo, the company's money. Total enjoyment on my first trip, my second, my third, maybe... but after that, most were drudgeries. As you know, there was a chapter on Japan, and since you enjoyed that chapter, I thought maybe I'd write about my other travels... don't worry there are only a few.

Anyway, I never had hot sauce on eggs.

What?

Could you just sit back and read? Your interruptions are becoming a nuisance.

It was the 1980s. I was on a business trip to a Silicon Valley company with a team to discuss computer-generated voice technology. Yes, we were into that forty years ago. We were to meet the company's lead designer, Shigeru Miyamoto, the inventor of Donkey Kong. I was totally pumped.

I loved playing Donkey Kong, thrilled every time I reached the next screen. The game was mesmerizing, very low-tech in today's world of gaming, yet still one of the all-time great video games. If you haven't seen the 2007 documentary film, *The King of Kong: A Fist Full of Quarters*, watch it. You'll love it.

Before our team drove to the meeting, we had breakfast outside on the hotel's pool deck.

"What are you doing to your eggs?" I asked Stan, our marketing guy, as he sprinkled hot sauce over his scrambled eggs.

"Without a little kick, eggs are dull. You should try some." He handed the bottle of Cholula to me.

I was intrigued and wanted to be part of team, so I dribbled some of the red molten fluid onto a corner of my eggs. My mom was a wonderful cook, but she treated spices like an unnecessary, maybe an immoral, thing.

"Really. That's all you are using?" The marketing guy said, picking up a forkful of his eggs, freckled with red sauce.

You guessed it. I loved it, and added more drops.

At the Silicon Valley company, Miyamoto strolled into the ten o'clock meeting, an hour and fifteen minutes late. His jet black hair was in ponytail, he wore a wrinkled

110

Hawaiian shirt, shorts, and flip-flops, and seemed a bit groggy. It was a short meeting, he had another one at ten-thirty.

The team returned to McDonnell Douglas with not much more insight into voice technology than when we left, but for me, it was a totally successful trip—I experienced hot sauce on eggs and shook the hand of the guy who created Donkey Kong. By the way, he took a job at Nintendo, where he created the *Mario* series of games, the *Legend of Zelda*, and others. He eventually became the gaming director at Nintendo, and probably dressed more conservatively.

That was interesting.

Thanks, There's three more… three interesting stories.

I visited England a few times during my career. On one trip, I was in London with a quality engineer and a marketing guy to visit the plant that produced the electronic tube for my Head up Display project. After seeing all the touristy sights, we sat down for dinner at Bentleys, a few blocks from Harrods's. Our table gave us a view of the car and foot traffic on Brompton Road.

The meals had just been delivered to our table, when a wailing siren filled the air; a firetruck roared past the restaurant.

"That must be a huge fire," I said as another truck and two police cars thundered by our window.

"Hope it's not our hotel," the marketing guy said, raising his pint of lager in the air.

We clicked glasses.

You guessed it. It was our hotel, which was about three blocks from the restaurant. My stomach lurched, when I saw firemen milling about, and the guests, some shoeless, some in robes, huddled on the sidewalk beyond the police tape. No smoke or flames to be seen. The police told us that it had been a kitchen fire, and it was nearly extinguished. Hours later, we were back in our rooms. It was one o'clock in the morning there, I think. I was a bit jet-lagged and lager-filled.

Back at work at the electronics company, I told the story to my workmates, and "Hope it's not our hotel" was a phrase when spoken, elicited laughter all around—childish but fun.

Yes, juvenile.

Anyway, wearing a hazmat suit is not fun.

Really? I could have told you that.

I was fortunate to be selected as a member of the Air Force Blue Team and was able to travel to Okinawa and South Korea. No, I was not a member of the *Air Force.* The Blue Team was a group of engineers from different companies that had equipment on Air Force bases around the world. The purpose of the trip was to experience your products in action, ask questions and get feedback on its usefulness from the operators. I was proud to have had a hand in designing the McDonnell Douglas test equipment that was installed on the airbase. It performed flawlessly, and the airmen loved it.

One morning the team assembled outside a hanger on Kunsan Air Force Base in South Korea. We stood facing a parked McDonnell Douglas F-15 Fighter—the sun was reflecting off the cockpit glass and the remove-before-flight tags were waving in the breeze. I have always enjoyed seeing the F-15—an extraordinary aircraft with incredible longevity. (On July 13, 2020, the Air Force awarded Boeing a nearly $1.2 billion contract for the first lot of the new F-15EX fighter jets.)

"Each company's rep will don a hazmat suit and remove

a piece of cockpit equipment," the base commander announced. "It's regular training exercise for our men, so... no problem." He paused and scanned the team. "Since we'll be working on the F-15, I thought the McDonnell Douglas engineer should go first."

The flag on hanger's roof went limp, as did I.

I was hoping the team members would be selected alphabetically and maybe time would run out before the S's were called.

I stepped forward when he called my name.

Donning the hazmat suit, sans the head covering, was easy, but the boots and gloves were a struggle; they were the biggest I'd ever seen. One of the airmen eased the headgear onto my head and sealed it to the suit. I was to climb a metal ladder, only about five steps, lean into the cockpit, and with a wench, extract the black box and insert a new one. Easy peasy I told myself, but not believing a word of it.

I gripped the handrails and struggled to lift my boot-enclosed foot onto each narrow step. I felt like the Hulk climbing up a ladder on Barbie's Dream House. Sweat was running down my face. I felt like I was losing pounds by the minute. I leaned into the cockpit, ready to extract the black box, when I heard the base commander yell, "Next!"

It turned out, the exercise was for the team members to only experience what it felt like to wear the suit and move around the aircraft, not actually maintain the equipment.

On the last day, the Blue Team went to the DMZ—the guarded strip of land between North and South Korea—about thirty miles from Seoul. Seeing the soldiers carrying guns and patrolling the DMZ was scary even though we were a *safe* distance away.

Those Korean patrols reminded me of my trip to Israel.

The American Airline aircraft did not taxi to the Ben Gurion Airport Terminal 3 but stopped on the tarmac. I stepped out of the plane onto the portable stairs to a startling sight. A gauntlet of Uzi-armed Israeli soldiers and psychologists (I learned later) stood at the base of the stairs.

I walked between the two lines of observers, keeping my eyes straight ahead, hoping my nervousness did not identify me as a terrorist. Inside the airport, everyone's luggage was opened and inspected, and my tighty-whities were there for all to see. Outside the airport, I was picked up by a driver, hired by the Israeli company I was to visit, who took me to the hotel.

Before traveling to Israel, I was briefed that my hotel room should be on the second floor, not facing the sea. You guessed it. My room was on the top floor with a beautiful view of the sparkling waters of the Mediterranean. I guess the McDonnell Douglas booking agency didn't get the word.

Why was the room location so important?

In my briefing, I was told that if there was a terrorist attack, it would be by sea and into the first floor. Therefore, a second floor room would allow the best chance of an escape.

Anyway, the Israeli company provided a driver and guide for me to see the local sights—the Dead Sea, Masada, Bethlehem, Wailing Wall, and other ancient places. Oh, by the way, business was also successfully conducted.

Joining the Israeli engineers for food and drinks were memorable experiences, but two dinners stood out. One was a private feast on the Mediterranean beach, and the other was at a restaurant next to the Sea of Galilee. At that restaurant, I ordered St. Peter's Fish. Well... the *entire* fish rested on the plate. Its eye, looking at me so sadly, made it difficult to eat. Even though the eye didn't blink and the tail didn't wiggle, I still only picked at it as I stared at the sea.

I had many company trips throughout the US, some memorable, most unremarkable, but I won't bore you with them, and... thanks for reading this chapter.

I'm glad you added your travel stories. It wasn't that bad.

10-4 GOOD BUDDY

Wait! Is 10-4 another engineering term?

No. I wouldn't bore with… oh right, I guess I have done that. 10-4 is part of the title of the chapter. It means… just read on.

Okay.

At the electronics company, we celebrated Broderick Crawford Day in a big way. Before you interrupt me again, let me explain because I'm sure most of my readers are saying "Huh?" But as you guessed—it is a dinosaur thing.

During the late 1950s, the TV show, *Highway Patrol*, starred Broderick Crawford as Dan Matthews, a gruff and dedicated head of the police force in a small western town. While leaning on his black and white patrol car, he barked rapid-fire dialogue into a radio microphone—way before cellphones were ever a gleam in the brain of some now wealthy engineer. After Broderick finished speaking, he'd always say 10-4, which meant *message end*. It was his signature catch phrase. Reflecting back on the TV show, it was cheesy as compared to today's programs. It had—lots of car chases, bloodless cartoon-style fighting, and cliché-filled dialogue—and was sponsored by a beer company. But man, was it popular.

Back to the electronics company, the Broderick Crawford Day celebration was on October 4th—get it,

10-4. I don't recall the first of this annual celebration, but I know that Carl, an electrical engineer, took responsibility for the festivities. The centerpiece of the event was a cake, a half-sheet cake decorated with a highway, trees, plastic people and cars, and of course, Broderick's signature patrol car. Over the years, the celebration became highly anticipated and drew bigger crowds.

Near the end of our time in Building 500, people were transferring to other departments and projects were being canceled, but Carl squeezed in one last Broderick Crawford Day celebration.

On the morning of October 4th, I saw Carl and another engineer carrying in a white cakebox with an oversized lid.

"Hey, Carl. That looks bigger than the others," I called out to him.

Carl didn't respond, only smiled.

I followed the guys into the conference room, the standard location for the festivities.

Carl and the other engineer carefully eased the cakebox onto the table, as if the box held delicate electronic parts. "This one is going to be special," Carl said. Then he turned to me and added, "Could you put a do-not-disturb sign on the door? We'll need some time to set up."

We always took a break at 10 a.m. on October 10th to make the celebration more special. "Is it still starting at the same time?" I asked in anticipation.

"Yes. Of course, it is."

At about five to ten, a crowd gathered in front of the closed conference room door. Many peopled asked, "What's going on in there?" No one was sure, but all expected an epic celebration—including me.

At ten on the dot—engineers are always accurate—

118

the door opened. Flashing lights could be seen in the darkened room.

The cake had blinking red and green lights along the chocolate highway. Crowds of plastic people stood on green icing and some gathered around a black and white patrol car resting on its top.

Before anybody could say anything, Carl said, "Thanks for coming and supporting this annual event. You may think that it's the end, but it's not. Broderick was involved in an accident, but he's okay. The doctor says he'd be back on the road before you know it."

Everyone cheered. It was like a comic-con event—it was all make-believe, and everyone enjoyed it. Oh, and the cake was always delicious.

That was interesting, but…

Yes, and even today, Broderick Crawford posts appear on Facebook on October 4th, mainly from former electronic company employees.

Anyway, this celebration was yet another example of the tight-knit, family-type group we had at the electronics company and marked another dinosaur ritual.

Wait! Don't leave us hanging. What flavor was the cake? Where did Carl buy it? What…

That's it. 10-4 my good readers.

IN CONCLUSION

Isn't this book long enough?
Probably, but I have to wrap things up.

First of all, there were so many people I worked with who made my job enjoyable, and I thought about mentioning all of them. In fact, I had a chapter where I was going to list all of my workmates, but my editor told me that wasn't a good idea because I would surely omit some.

Thank goodness for editors.

But I am very thankful for every person I interfaced with at the electronics company. They made my times there gratifying.

Secondly, I want to say that I totally enjoyed my career as an electronic engineer—somehow I chose the right profession. Also, I am proud to have worked at McDonnell Douglas, on hi-tech projects, alongside of some great people who became my friends, and whom I miss today. That's enough of that. I don't want to get maudlin.

I'm happy you had an enjoyable career.

Thanks, now let's get back to the conclusion.

I love the stage production and the movie, *Fiddler on the Roof*, and the song, *Tradition*. Tradition is a belief or behavior passed down within a group or society with symbolic meaning or special significance with origins in the past.

Wow! You're still defining stuff.

Yep. As I said before—it's an engineer's thing.

Does following tradition make you a dinosaur? Some would argue—absolutely not. Tradition preserves heritage, and that's a good thing. Others would say—we need to break with tradition, move on, and forge our own path.

Another thought, does being overcome by events make you a dinosaur? Maybe. For example, you might have promised yourself you would try a sport, a hobby, an art or a craft. Now you find you are up to your ears in parenting, or overcome by business commitments, or enjoying retirement, or have lost the physical dexterity or stamina to take on a new sporting activity.

That paragraph doesn't seem to fit... but let me think about it.

Dinosaur activities could have grown from habits. We all have habits—some you may want to break and others you want to keep. You might think you understand a habit, but you can never exactly see what it looks like when you're doing it, like others do. I'm not thinking about smoking, but more like men and women wearing their hair in a long-gone style.

And being a dinosaur is not age-related. For example, the people, who continued to make buggy whips while cars took over the roads, the people who believe coal is the fuel of tomorrow while reusable energy is at our doorstep, and people who cling to gas-powered cars while hybrids and all-electric cars populate the streets, are dinosaurs. Some of my friends are proud that they have no computer skills and don't own a smart phone—a typical dinosaur mantra.

My dad would enjoy a cup of coffee as he read the morning newspaper, and I do the same, even though I have an iPhone, iPad, and a desktop PC—all accessible to the news. Besides getting the daily newspaper—basically to read Dilbert and work the NYT crossword puzzle—I also have to admit that I have a landline, not sure why, but it's a dinosaur thing.

What clothes you wear and how you wear them, could classify you as a dinosaur. One morning I glanced into the mirror—I had my shirt tucked inside my jeans. I pulled it out, trying to be more modern. I looked bloated. I smoothed the shirt and still didn't like the look. So... I rarely go untucked—a definite dinosaur style.

I am trying to avoid extinction for as long as I can, like keeping up with technology, making short- and long-term goals, and eating right—although an empty bag of Chili-Cheese Fritos occasionally appears in the wastebasket.

Well, that's it my dear reader...

Wait! So, we'll all dinosaurs?

Yes, admit it or not, we're all dinosaurs in some way, obvious or not, and some more noticeable than others. We hang on to things from our past, knowingly or unknowingly. And after reading this book, you may have identified dinosaur traits in yourself. It's not a bad thing, but I wouldn't flaunt it.

Anyway, I hope you have enjoyed the jaunt through my working days, found it humorous in some spots, some topics interesting, and others not too boring. I have enjoyed telling you about my career and hope you... Oh. Excuse me. I have a call on my landline.

ACKNOWLEDGEMENTS

Thanks to my workmates who gather at the Corner Bar on the second Wednesday of every month. Over pitchers of beer, burgers and onion rings, we share memories of projects, company characters, and escapades at the electronics company in Building 500. Their stories jogged my memory about my experiences at work and beyond.

Thanks to Sharon St Moritz for taking over for me as the organizer of the reunions and for her comments on the characters in my book.

Thanks to Jim Rehg, my co-author of our college textbooks, for our conversations about writing and his critiques of my works.

Thanks to my friends at the St. Louis Writers Guild for their support and encouragement.

Thanks to Karen Sargent, for her insightful critique on my book description.

Thanks to Jennifer Carson for the design of the cover and for designing and building the interior for the Kindle and paperback versions. She has been there with me for all of my books, from the first one—Epiphany, published in 2013 by her company—to this most recent one.

And my deepest thanks to my wife, Rosanne, a published author, for her insightful comments and edits to my narratives. It's a better book because of her.

ABOUT THE AUTHOR

Glenn Sartori has written mystery novels and memoirs plus electrical engineering textbooks for the college and trade school markets. He lives in St. Louis with his wife, Rosanne. His *Never Knew I Was a Dinosaur* memoir is an entertaining follow up to his South City Mosaic trilogy.

Visit him at his website: www.glennsartori.com

Made in the USA
Coppell, TX
30 October 2020

40535563R00075